Bob & Jos Mahon

Barney's Long Walk

Backpacking Land's End to John o' Groats

off road with a dog

(or '*The Wet 'n Wild Way!*')

GW00506980

Barney's Long Walk

www.hudsridingpress.co.uk

Printed by Mixam UK Ltd.

Contents

Preface

By Bob Mahon

Walking from Land's End to John o' Groats, tramping endless miles on roads was never on my list of 'things to do'. That changed in 2007 when a keen backpacker documented his attempt online and a guidebook was published describing an off-road route. I then read John Hillaby's seminal 1968 book of the challenge 'Journey Through Britain' and was inspired.

My wife Jos and I enjoy long distance backpacking in remote locations. Our expeditions are as much as possible off-road. It is necessary to carry everything you need to survive in places such as the Scottish Highlands.

An Teallach from Loch an Nid

I realised from the guide that it was possible to backpack LEJOG in the way we enjoy. In 2015 the opportunity arose for us to attempt it and we took up the challenge.

Why 'Barney's Long Walk'? Our faithful canine companion Barney, a flatcoat retriever, always accompanied us on expeditions. Carrying panniers, he regularly attracts attention, so we decided to take advantage of this to raise money for Guide Dogs. To many online followers, he became an important part of the adventure.

Jos's diary forms the basis of this book, usually written in the tent every evening after the long days walk. It gives a good insight into a challenge of this nature. This includes coming to terms, after only a few days into our trek, with bad news. Archie, our youngest grandson in Australia, was diagnosed with a tumour. Following this shock, we had ongoing doubts about whether to continue the walk. Should we instead travel across the world to be of help to our overseas and distant family?

We have included many of the photographs taken as we walked. These show the ever changing landscape we experienced as we made our way north.

Jos, being an artist, painted en route, producing a 'visual' diary of the trip as it progressed. This, in itself was a major undertaking as is described in the following pages. Reduced size representations of some of the paintings are included[*].

Morven viewed from the Knockfin Heights

* For a more complete representation, Jos has produced another book,
  'Painting on the End to End Trail' ISBN: 978-1-8384640-1-1

Introduction

By Jos Mahon

In Spring 2015, we (that's me, husband Bob and our dog Barney) set off from Land's End in Cornwall to walk all the way up to the other end of Britain, to John o' Groats in Caithness. We wanted to do the End to End, also called LEJOG (Land's End to John o' Groats), before we all got too old! In our case it was 'when we were 64' and Barney, 8.

We are experienced back packers, having walked and camped many multi day trips in the Scottish Highlands and climbed all the Munros (284 Scottish mountains 3000ft and higher) over the years, but had never attempted a trip this long before and it took a lot of planning.

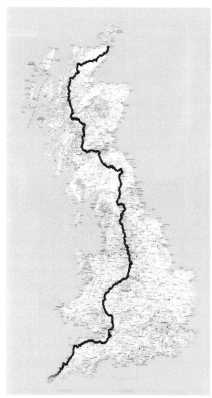

The Route

The route we chose, mostly followed 'The End to End Trail', a Cicerone guide written by Andy Robinson. He goes 'off road', avoiding tarmac as much as possible, following footpaths, tracks and National Trails and in Scotland over challenging pathless terrain. We liked Andy's idea of taking to the hills and wilder parts of the country, experiencing on foot such a variety of scenery – coastal cliffs, mountains and moorland, farmland, hills and dales, woodland, rivers and canals. Our walk was a long one, totalling nearly 1,400 miles, taking us about 4 months altogether. We were following spring north, with early flowers in abundance in Cornwall and Devon at the end of March; daffodils still flowering in the North Pennines in June.

The weather was very changeable with a lot of rain throughout the journey, gales and gusts on Cornish cliff tops, sleet on the longest day, the 21st June, in the Cheviot hills. We also experienced a couple of short heat-waves, one not long after we started, in Devon, and then again in the Scottish Central Belt (heat proved to be the most challenging of weather conditions for walking, as we are not used to it, coming from Northumberland).

Wild camp, Glen Finglas

We camped most of the way, because we love it, especially wild camping, this mostly in Scotland, pitching the tent next to streams in the hills where you experience the solitude and sounds of a mountain glen. In England and Wales we used small camp sites, enjoying the luxury of a shower and chance to wash clothes, but there were times when we spent the night in a field, or perched on a cliff top. We used B&B's only a few times, and they were in very characterful, quite special old pubs, including The Harbour Inn, Clovelly, Devon, The Tan hill Inn, North Yorkshire[*] and the most remote – The Crask Inn, Sutherland.

We never booked ahead, preferring the freedom of 'seeing how we get on and how far we've got'. A most enjoyable part of the trip was catching up with and spending the night with friends and family as we made our progress up the country, experiencing such kindness and help with all kinds of logistics. We also made friends on the way and met with warm generosity and assistance from complete strangers.

* The highest in England

4

Barney

Photo by: Dean Sawyer

Our dog Barney became a star on the trip which became known as 'Barney's Long Walk'. I don't know whether any other dog has walked the route we took. He has been our constant companion on our walks in local Pennine and Cumbrian fells and on camping / backpacking trips in Scotland. He has enjoyed many an adventure and as he was fit, there was no question that he would accompany us on our long walk.

Our local vet was concerned about whether his paws would cope with all the walking. As a precaution, every morning I anointed his paws with a special Canadian paw cream used on huskies. When we walked on tarmac cycle paths in a heatwave, it was our feet that suffered, not Barney's!

On previous backpacking trips, Barney had been used to carrying his share of the load, his own food, treats, first aid, dog towel, in dog panniers on his back. People meeting us would invariably stop and smile and ask what he was carrying, our food? - our beer? etc. Knowing that he would attract this attention on the way, we had the idea at a late

Barney's harness and panniers

stage in our planning, that he could try raising funds for Guide Dogs.

Initially, we had no plans to do the walk for charity like many do, most of whom take the shortest route on roads. We were doing it for our own challenge and pleasure. However Barney's fund raising for Guide Dogs gave us so much unforeseen enjoyment and interest as we walked. From the very

5

beginning at Land's End where a guide dog owner and her dog came especially to meet us and wish us well, we learnt just how special and life changing a guide dog is to a blind or partially sighted person. We met up with guide dog trainers and puppy walkers, some walking a short distance with us. It added an unexpected dimension to the walk which we really enjoyed.

Whenever people stopped to ask what he was carrying, we fell into conversation about what we were undertaking. We gave them cards with details about Barney's blog and Facebook page which Bob managed to keep up from the tent at night, given signal and power. We gave out over 700 cards advertising what Barney was doing...

It was amazing how many people began following our progress online, many saying how they were learning about the country from the comforts of their armchair every night. Donations came from people we met and online via a JustGiving page. Things snowballed, and a fantastic spin off due to Barney clocking up the miles was 'Match a Mile for Barney', a scheme initiated by Dogs Unite, a fund-raising arm of the Guide Dogs charity. This involved 1,200 dog owners (our initial expected total mileage) taking their own dogs on sponsored walks adding many thousands of pounds to the total raised.

Barney is a flatcoated retriever, a breed known for such a friendly, joyful, enthusiastic, people loving disposition and he naturally attracted attention on the walk anyway, but especially from other flatcoat owners. We got him from the flatcoat rescue and re-homing scheme when he was young and very boisterous, he soon took to our active lifestyle with typical gusto.

When we left Land's End in March, we had no idea what a star he would become by the time we reached John o' Groats 4 months later. Of course in our eyes he was a star already!

Painting en Route

For me, an artist, a major element of the walk was making paintings all the way, chronicling the journey visually, personally, wherever I was, whatever the weather. I wanted to convey the feel of the countryside we walked through and work in the wind and rain.

Gales, Gusts, Wild Day

Oddly, I find summer sun more difficult, but that was not to be a problem; I had thought I might paint every single day, but sometimes the weather really was just too wet, too windy or even too hot!

Sometimes I record the length of walking day was just too long, and often wrote in my diary, lamenting lost sketching opportunities where I could have stopped and painted, but got to press on…

I am an artist whose inspiration is the outdoors. For many years I have filled sketchbooks with rapidly painted responses to place and weather. I have worked in remote landscapes from Pennines to Scottish Highlands and Islands, and on epic treks in Iceland, Greenland, New Zealand and Nepal.

For our long walk, packing painting equipment was as essential and natural to me as the first aid kit, food and camping stove. I was determined to paint all the way, every day if I could, knowing from past experience that the chance to work would be fleeting, snatched during a rest / lunch break.

Preparing paper packs

As with route and equipment preparation, organising for a 4 month painting expedition took some careful planning. I decided to make up my own sketch-pads, cutting up sheets of different types of robust watercolour paper to a panoramic format 6" x 15". I used tough rubber bands to hold about 20 together with a piece of card as backing, plus the essential waterproof plastic bag to keep the package dry. From a practical point of view, the rubber bands held the edges of the paper while I worked, then I slipped the completed page to the back, often still damp, keeping good hold so it did not blow away. It was well worth using robust paper, experimenting with a variety of types.

This shape jammed down the back length of my rucksack helping provide additional padding. Along with a bag of minimal materials, paints, brushes and pencils, it was all extra weight to carry.

Bob carried a second package of paper for me, and when both 'books' were used up, I posted them home. I picked more up which we had posted ahead

8

to family, friends and camp-sites along with other essentials and maps as we made our way north.

Thankfully, they all arrived safely home, well weather worn from the various stages of the walk, together forming a large body of work documenting our journey up the length of Great Britain. In the course of the trip, I made about 280 paintings and drawings.

Ingleborough and Pen-y-ghent edge

They convey the constantly changing colours and shapes of the land we moved through along with the effects of working at speed in often challenging weather conditions, when only the essentials can be put down. Many are spattered with raindrops and dead midges.

An artist friend requested a painted postcard to be sent once a week, showing our progress. I endeavoured to produce the cards – a small painting along with a message and these are included in the following diary.

Card to be sent off and a panoramic view to carry

Weather and Route

Damp conditions at the start

When we left Land's End in Cornwall at the end of March, we were in full winter gear, dressed for Scotland. Cornish mizzle (mist and drizzle) turned to over a week of heavy rain and gale force winds, blowing me over at one point on the cliff path we were taking. It made for challenging painting conditions with rain soaked water colours.

Dramatic coastal scenery, Cornwall

A complete change to a settled, early April heatwave, made for arduous walking up and down the high Cornish and Devon dramatic headlands. Out came the blues and turquoise colours of sea and sky and white pounding surf, exciting after the muted washed out greys of our start.

Lots of ups and downs

We struggled in the heat on leaving the SWCP[*], heading inland for Barnstaple and suffered major blister problems walking on the scorching tarmac cycle track to get there.

The heat continued as we hiked up onto the Exmoor hills where finding enough water to drink became an issue. Not for long though as from then on, unsettled weather became the norm as we crossed the Quantock hills, down to the fen-like, cow rich Somerset levels, climbed Cheddar gorge and the Mendips to drop down to the misty Bristol Channel.

Here we crossed the river Severn, heads down as rain swept across the long road bridge, to enter Wales at Chepstow and met the swollen brown river Wye. I noted in my diary: 'Wales is very wet and very green', with woods full of bluebells on our route following the hilly Offa's Dyke path along the Welsh border as far as Knighton.

I loved the heady views of the Black Mountains from a high ridge walk, where we walked in wind and showers.

* South West Coast Path

11

The Hatterrall Ridge in the Welsh Borders

The weather settled again as we turned north east for Herefordshire, Shropshire and Staffordshire, a rich mix of agricultural land, green pasture grazed by sheep and lambs, woodland full of flowers atop Wenlock Edge.

Midlands farming country

We crossed the Severn once more at historic Ironbridge, following footpaths around crops and ploughed fields, along tow-paths of peaceful canals, yet all the while a step away from busy motorways and conurbations. For me, used to painting the windswept dark brown Pennine moors, the many greens and rural lushness of this part of the country with blue skies was a complete change.

Gradually as we began a northerly line from Uttoxeter, following the river Dove, we entered limestone country. On hearing the first curlew since leaving home we began to feel we were back in the hills, our internal compass set north, with rock outcrops, stone walls and rain again.

At last we reached the Pennine Way, high open moors and long horizons, a corridor of land squeezing between conurbations, bleak, windswept country crossed east west by busy roads. The M62, came and went.

First day on the Pennine Way, Sandy Heys

I felt in my element, with a sheer sense of exhilaration from striding along on the upland areas, out in wind and rain and the excitement of nearing home.

Still a long way to go, more dramatic features; the limestone cove at Malham; onwards to the steep outlined rocky edges of the Yorkshire 3 peaks: Pen-y-ghent, Ingleborough and Whernside. End of May now and winter gloves and hat bought at Horton in Ribblesdale for more elemental weather, gales and heavy rain.

It was emotionally moving, reaching the top of Shunner Fell from Hawes, to gaze across to the Eden valley and Cross Fell, familiar shapes of the hills of home.

The River Tees at High Force

A surprising respite from cold rain, when a few days later, we walked the flower filled meadows alongside the river Tees in the warmth of the sun. A day later, early June, gales rain and cold, as we fought our way up Cross Fell, to spend a freezing night in the mountain bothy Greg's Hut on the flanks of the highest hill on the Pennine Way. From the 'comforts' of a hut indoor window I was able to spend time painting the light ebbing away over the northern horizons. Next day it was a struggle to stay upright walking just as it had been back in March on the Cornish cliffs in gale force wind.

We departed from the Pennine way at Garrigill near Alston and made straight for home at Catton, near Allendale where we had an unforeseen break, as we recovered from bad colds. Ironically it was a change to warm weather at home, only to start raining again as we resumed our walk to finish the Pennine way on the Scottish border at Kirk Yetholm. That was the day we had sleet showers on the high Cheviot hills on June 21st – the longest day!

The Scottish border from wild camp

Once in the Scottish Borders, the colours changed from the dark browns of Pennine peat to a rich green with grass growing to the hilltops around Jedburgh and Melrose.

In Scotland for the next 6 to 7 weeks, from the end of June to the beginning of August, it rained most days which at least kept the infamous irritating Scottish midge away. We did, however, enjoy odd days of fine sunshine when wet gear hung on the backs of rucksacks to dry as we walked along. There was even a 3 day mini 'heat wave' just at the time we were walking on hard surfaced canal tow-paths through the Central Belt. From here on we were mostly wild camping, following our own route through the Trossachs to Killin and on to Fort William.

When pitched in Glen Finglas (north of Brig o' Turk) above the loch, just us, Canada geese on the water below, clouds over the mountain tops, I felt very happy and content, at last back in the Highlands. I began a series of paintings from inside the tent looking out across the loch before bed. Interestingly, the daily tally of paintings now increased as there was so much to feel inspired by and longer hours of daylight on this last stage of our journey.

Heading towards Fort William

After Killin, in Perthshire, our way was pathless, up over remote bealachs,[*] wild camping on mountain sides; on Rannoch moor and through remote boggy glens in torrential rain to reach Fort William where it was unusually sunny.

Loch Lochy and Ben Nevis

* Mountain passes

A fine day along our last canal tow-path (the Caledonian) before more wild, wet and remote camping, always next to water; by lochs and burns in glens all the way up to Glen Affric, Kinlochewe and the Torridon mountains and on to Ullapool on the north west coast. Much to inspire, when the rain ceased and there was a chance to paint.

Liathach & Shoulder of Beinn Eighe

During our rest weekend in Ullapool, camped by the shore, it was ridiculously sunny, blue sky, holiday, ice cream weather and stunning coastal sunsets. Not for long the fine weather, as we made our way in more days of showers up the side of the river Oykel.

Remote Lands – looking across to Ben More Assynt

We turned north east under the brooding shoulder of Ben More Assynt, aiming for the boggy Flow country of Sutherland and Caithness, leaving high mountains behind. After stopping at the remote Crask Inn, we continued our wild camping until finally reaching the north east coast at the Bay of Sinclair, Keiss.

Bealach Easach and the end of the mountains

We were rewarded on our final day of walking by fine, dry, sunny, fresh and breezy weather as we made our way along dramatic cliff edges up to the stacks at Duncansby Head. We could walk north no longer.

The Stacks of Dunscanby

The land ends, the Orkney islands lie on the northern horizon. We turned left, west for the John o' Groats campsite, our journey's end.

Diary and Blog entries

This book is a combination of my diary and Bob's blog entries, both written daily, normally after we had finished walking and erected the tent. At this time, Bob was getting a brew on and attempting to update social media; Barney was normally asleep at my feet as shown in the picture...

We have divided the daily entries into 6 sections, matching the guidebook structure. Each section first has an overall description followed by the daily entries. We have made changes to our original entries only where necessary. One comment on the blog referred to the number of exclamation marks so we have removed many! Bob's blog entries were mostly short general descriptions whilst I was able to make a more personal record of our exploits.

Each day entry includes 3 sections:

1. Information for the day including the destination, miles walked and height ascent.
2. Blog postings.
3. My end of day diary notes.

We didn't mention grandson Archie's cancer diagnosis in the blog or on the Facebook page as we felt this was a personal, family worry.

Our Facebook and Blog reports included daily miles walked taken from the gps. The distances included here are as calculated in our mapping software and typically a mile or so shorter each day. So we walked nearly 1400 miles according to the gps and 1330 miles according to the computer!

Interspersed between diary entries are small sections added by Bob which give some details on various aspects of the trip.

We often mention family and friends by name, with footnotes to show who they are.

Planning

The trip gradually took shape over a number of years but preparation only really began after New Year 2015. Things started to take shape in February, less than two months before we were due to leave – kit checked, re-supply parcels sent off and all the other tasks that go into making a trek of this length possible.

Organising something of this nature doesn't always run smoothly (at least it didn't for us) and we had several problems just before we started.

First, Barney had a lump appear on his nether parts requiring urgent visits to the vets and following remedial action – an operation. It was benign but would he be able to walk for 3 months and more after such an event? After consultation we decided that it was possible but would have to be prepared to change plans if necessary.

Then, we lost our prospective house sitter due to a communications misunderstanding. As you may imagine, finding somebody to live in your house for 3 months starting in under 2 weeks could potentially be a problem. We did have a contingency plan partially sorted – friends would take on the basic tasks of looking after 2 cats and 4 hens. This however meant the house being unoccupied for long periods of time – not ideal and had associated insurance problems. I set to on social media and soon had names of potential occupants. Within a few hours we had this problem resolved with a local couple moving in when we left, quite happy to have the space which our house offered.

The time soon passed and come 26th March all we had to do was get to the start…

26th March. Haydon Bridge – Penzance by train

On the train south and it was snowing as we left.
11 hours on trains was quite enough. Barney was the topic of many conversations and one unfortunate man even missed the station he was supposed to get off at.
Another conversation resulted in a £10 donation

Haydon Bridge 7am

It was snowing when we left at 6:30am for the station, with dear friend Rosie giving us a lift. She gave me a lovely card with a line of a Celtic prayer *'May the wind be ever in your back'* which will be the case tomorrow as gales are forecast. Newcastle felt freezing. On the 'plane like' train whizzing down country through York, Leeds, Sheffield, Birmingham and Bristol, Barney took up the centre aisle. I moved him into the end corridor every time the trolley and people came.

People were so friendly, we chatted with a man who missed his stop because he was so keen on talking to us!

Journey went fine – Barney was brilliant, calm, up and down in the narrow aisle to Plymouth then a very crowded old train to Penzance. Through Devon hills and Cornish fields, some full of daffodils, people chat because of the dog. One woman gave us £10. He was so good, flat out now in the tent and we are tired too, on our way at last. It's a stormy night after a fine sunny day – contrast to this mornings cold wet snow.

Penzance campsite 7am next day

Here we are in the tent 8:20pm in a secluded lawn area of a very quiet Bone Valley Caravan And Camping Park, Penzance, after lovely fish & chips (just made it before 7pm close) - 'There you are my lovely'. All very friendly and campsite lady made us mugs of tea and sat us in the camp lounge for our fish supper.

Tomorrow morning, all we have to do is catch the bus to Land's End and start walking...

Section 1. The South West Coast Path

Land's End to Barnstaple

2 nights wild camp, 2 nights with relatives, 1 pub and 14 nights campsites   **189 miles**

Very variable weather – wild and windy through to baking hot and sunny   **38147 ft**

This first stage of the route follows the South West Coast Path, along spectacular cliffs, with a lot of climbing up to headlands and back down to coves and sandy bays.

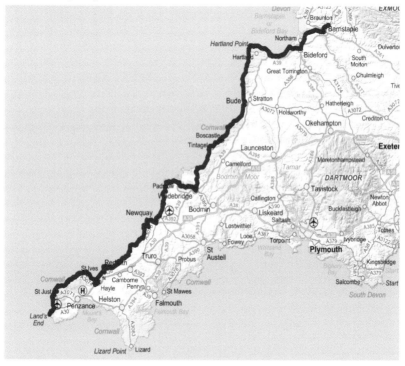

Following the SWCP*, we had a challenging start to our long walk due to terrain and weather conditions. We set off on cliff paths with rugged steep ascents and descents, crashing seas on our left sides. A Cornish mizzle set in as soon as I sat to do my first paintings at Sennen Cove. Thick sea fog

*South West Coast Path

descended. Tall, derelict chimneys, relics of tin mining era loomed up out of the mist. Over the next few days, gale force winds got up with dangerous gusts especially when we reached exposed headlands. We had to use our poles for balance. I did get blown over once. Fortunately it was an onshore wind. Tents blew down at St. Ives. Our small mountain tent stayed up. I painted when I could, on reaching more sheltered bays or tucked in behind a rock. We looked back at headlands we had walked, disappearing into mist, ahead lay more stunning coast.

After 8 days, the weather changed, the wind dropped and a heat wave began. Days became hot and sunny, it felt like walking abroad, needing sun cream and wearing shorts. The heat was to be more problematic than gales, causing major blister problems at Barnstaple after hot tarmac walking, necessitating a break in our journey.

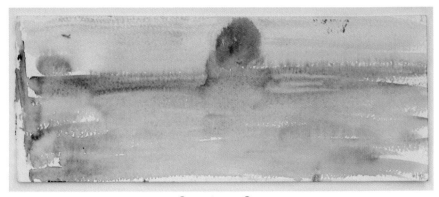
Sunset over Sea

The sea calmed down, even tranquil, enhanced colours, turquoise water, red cliffs. Without the roar of an accompanying wind, chance to notice birdsong, heralding springs arrival, migrants as the chiff-chaff, blackcap, willow warbler as well as wren and robin calling from the thorny scrub and thick bushes alongside the coastal path. Blackthorn in blossom, yellow gorse, and underfoot, banks of primroses, violets, red campion.

Evening light and chance to paint sunsets from cliff top camping, no longer 'battened down' inside the tent. My mantra became 'I could've stopped for more painting, but got to press on', as day after day we hiked up and down steep dramatic headlands in the heat.

Day 1 27/3 Land's End to Pendeen.

Camped in field next to North Inn, Pendeen	9.2 miles
Wet, misty, cold, thick fog	1847 ft

> *Great to be seen off by Nigel, Kay and her guide dog Jackie who Barney got on very well with. Off into the mizzle for our first day on the Cornish coast. Lots of mine shafts and chimneys, just like home. Good to camp next to pub, The North Inn at Pendeen.*

Dry start to pack up and walk downhill to Penzance and catch the double decker bus to Land's End *(couldn't use bus passes – too early).*

It was wet, misty and cold when we got off. We had a wander around the tourist complex which was all closed and deserted. We met up with Kay & Nigel Kitto, along with Kay's guide dog Jackie, all so pleased and excited for us. We spent 2 hours with them, having coffee, chat and photos at the signpost. Then it was time to begin.

It made a really good start seeing a guide dog owner loving and working with their dog. The independence it gives the owner, so important and worthwhile.

We met a young man at the start, about to cycle LEJOG and climb the 3 peaks, Snowdon etc. en route!

It all starts here… Photo by Nigel Kitto

Leaving Land's End

Lovely to see Sennen Bay with its very Opdahl* headlands. I had a go at painting from the beach in the mizzle. There were lots of ups and downs, rucksack a bit heavy after an hour or more.

Thick fog descended as we walked past old tin mines, shafts, buildings and huge chimneys right on the coast. Lots of shaft like caves for smugglers! It felt quite a trudge at end of day, in fog, over fields till we finally found the North Inn. Very friendly, and beer straight away, tent up, then back to the pub for huge meal, dry out and charge up *(Donations already).*

Barney was very tired.

* Ornulph Opdahl is a Norwegian artist

Day 2 28/3 Pendeen to St Ives

Ayr Holiday Park, St Ives	13.3 miles
Windy, wet start then dry and windy	3239 ft

An initially wet and finally very windy day. Path rugged with many ups and downs. Between showers, Jos still found time to paint. After the mistake of taking a 'short cut' on the last headland, we arrived at the campsite as the wind was increasing. A number of tents didn't survive the night.

A windy first night in the pub field, the tent very damp inside with condensation and outside very damp too. It was raining as we packed up. There was laughter from a man in the street at the weather! We found a shop to buy goodies for us and the dog.

Brief stop to sketch

We set off for Pendeen Watch lighthouse and turned east, with the wind at our backs – one headland after another. The rain stopped but clouds stayed on the hills.

I enjoyed the wildness even though the wind blew me over and my pack pulled me head first. Strong wind all day, but with walking poles I managed to keep upright in the gusts on the headlands. We then had steep descents.

All merged in memory now – saw only one house tucked away and I knocked to ask for a water refill. It looked a lovely place. We met just a few other walkers, no long distance ones. A coast to return to in the sunshine one day.

Wicca Bay

55 mph wind forecast for tomorrow. St Ives lies below us – looked Spanish from a distance – except not very blue. Hope to see some art as we walk through. So today, challenging, wild, elemental, lots of ascent.

Day 3 29/3 St Ives to Gwithian

Gwithian Farm Campsite	12.3 miles
Very windy night	1203 ft

A morning in St Ives including the Barbara Hepworth Museum and a surprise encounter with another flat coat. Then more ups and downs as we made our way around to Hayle, just getting to Asda before they shut at 4.
Dramatic walk along the beach to Gwithian – very similar to our Northumberland coast and another excellent camp site and pub. The wind has finally subsided – rain tomorrow...

British Summer Time begins today.

Heavy seas at St. Ives

Such a wild and windy night on the hilltop Ayr campsite. The tent was buffeted but we felt fully confident it would stay up. Could hear others having trouble and retreating to their cars. A German family camped next to us in another Hilleberg[*] tent. We gave them a card, also to the site lady and flatcoat owners we met in St Ives *(later noted they donated £50)*

Two Forms (Divided Circle)

St. Ives was busy, even people in the sea, surfing. I made straight for the Barbara Hepworth Museum.

Bob and Barney were let in to sit and wait in reception. The garden full of tropical type trees and foliage – an ideal setting for different styles of her sculpture, the early ones with holes, ribbons of steel. I liked the movement and rhythm. Her studio you could see through glass. I must have another read about her as I found her very inspiring when I was a sculpture student.

We moved on to sample our first Cornish pasty from a bakery, which was excellent. Standing by the harbour, we bumped into a family with a flatcoat, another large rangy looking one. We had a good chat with his owners, gave them a card and continued along the street to find excellent coffee, outdoors under cover. St. Ives – water, boats, beach, buildings and sky – looked very Nicholson[†] with shades of grey, slate, blue, sand…

Then we were off, after 1pm, following the coast path, up and down again, alongside beach (no dogs), railway line, sand dunes. Across the Hayle Estuary we could see the beach we'd walk later in the day. We hit lanes on the outskirts of Hayle, stretches of road, Barney getting tired and fed up.

* The same Swedish brand as our tent.
† Ben Nicholson – English abstract painter married to Barbara Hepworth

Where's my tea?

But hooray, we made it to Asda and Bob shopped in ¼ hour as it shut at 4pm, so lots of treats to keep us going. Barney needs them more now.

Finally a walk back north along the Hayle river, to reach a vast beach and empty sands with pounding waves on our left – reminding us of Northumberland. Barney enjoyed a play in the surf without his panniers.

I made a quick sketch of Godrevy Lighthouse[*] sited on a small rocky island.

At last, we made it to a great site, Gwithian Farm, where a friendly woman put us on a sheltered pitch for £12. Very good toilets and showers. It rained as we pitched in record time.

Had tea in tent, now sampling beer in nearby pub.

* Made famous by Virginia Woolf in her novel 'To the Lighthouse'

30

Day 4 30/3 Gwithian to Porthtowan

Porthtowan Tourist Park	13.2 miles
Sunny start, gale, gusts, wild night	2544 ft

Son of campsite owner took charge of coffee machine, made us an excellent brew. Friends who go out with Jos and Barney will recognise the painting pics – messy hands and Barney resting. Late in to campsite after making a mistake with the route.

Another long day with a challenging end as the campsite was closed, but phew, we were allowed in. The day started leisurely, we woke to sunshine and blue skies. We just didn't feel like rushing on, so we dried wet gear and washed things, then had a coffee before leaving the lovely site.

We met a couple and daughter Daisy from London who were taken with Barney and took a photo of us to put on Facebook.

Karolie and her golden retrievers

From the Godrevy headland, we looked across to the lighthouse. Further round, a view down to a cove full of hundreds of seals and pups. We chatted to a women, Karolie, with 3 golden retrievers. She lives in Cheddar and gave us her phone number, so we can stay with her. She used to teach at Alston only 10 miles from home.

Mucky work painting in the rain

It was a very enjoyable walk on cliff tops, rain keeping at bay, with great scenery at Hells Mouth, including stacks and pounding waves.

We walked on paths hugging the cliffs and I sketched another headland and stacks at Crane Islands.

Hell's Mouth

On to Bassets Cove, then dropped down to Portreath with a tiny harbour and wild seas outside. We went into a cafe for a very welcome mug of tea and brownie before the leg to Porthtowan. A gale got up and it became very wild, with gusts on the high cliffs. Steep downs and ups with steps. We had to use our poles a lot to balance against the gusts. All getting tired. We passed more derelict mine chimneys looking very dramatic in mist. Relieved to descend to Porthtowan only to discover we had to climb up a long steep hill to the campsite – well what campsite? The Eco one was as dead as a doornail and the other was closed. The friendly owner took pity on us, opened up a disabled toilet and said to find a sheltered spot. So here we are at Porthtowan Tourist Park, another late pitch and lucky too. It's 9:30pm, blowing a hooley, loud noise of trees, but tent not moving and we're all fed and watered – phew. Rang cousin Keith[*] to say we're all fine and looking forward to meeting him at Easter.

Porthtowan Tourist Park the following morning after a wild night

[*] Bob's cousin Keith and his wife Margaret live in Cornwall and kindly offered to put us up.

Our Worldly Goods for the Trek

For every long distance walker, the carried weight is, or will be, a central factor to the success (or otherwise) of the trek. Experience is the best guide in understanding just what is an acceptable weight to carry, too heavy and each day can become a struggle to get through. Most backpackers go through the process of weighing / reweighing and adding / discarding items until they achieve a load which is acceptable. With many items, decisions have to be made between weight and functionality. An ultralightweight tent for example may not have the strength and protection required when sitting out a day of strong winds and torrential rain. Lightweight walking boots are desirable but not if you end up with sore feet.

Every piece of kit is considered – is it actually needed, can its weight be reduced or can it be replaced with something lighter and smaller. Even toothbrush handles are cut back to reduce weight!

Food is another factor to consider when backpacking off-road and has a major influence on weight. We couldn't always guarantee we would be able to pick up supplies day by day as we weren't always near shops. This meant carrying food and restocking as and when we could. Our normal maximum was 4 days food which made for a heavy load at first, but became lighter each day as it was consumed.

Through many previous treks, we had learned just what the 3 of us (Barney carries a load as well) can and cannot carry. This trip however produced extra challenges in what was included in our loads.

We decided to carry a small amount of extra clothing over and above our normal minimum of hardly anything. Cameras and other technical equipment required us to carry batteries and additional hardware. All told, we estimated an increase in 2-4Kg over our normal maximum load. New rucksacks with more supportive frames and waist belts were obtained to carry the extra weight.

We realised early on that we were still carrying too much and so jettisoned some of the extra clothes as soon as possible. This meant the only spare clothes we were carrying consisted of underwear and socks along with our usual warm top for use in the morning and evening when camped. When our walking clothes needed washing we simply wore our wet weather gear instead.

Our base weights were about 11Kg for Jos and 13 Kg for Bob, with food adding 3 Kg at times. This included painting materials, but not water meaning a carry weight of 11-15Kg for Jos and 13-17Kg for Bob. See page 333 for details.

Barney carried up to 2Kg food plus additional bits and pieces although we lightened his load when he appeared to be flagging. It was remarkable however that he soon got a spring back in his step when the load was eased!

Day 5 31/3 Porthtowan to St Agnes

Bluehills campsite near St Agnes	6.9 miles
Sunny start, very windy, cold	1610 ft

A bracing, shorter day as we wanted to make camp before it was getting dark. Still superb coastline. Barney getting lots of treats. The response we've had over the last few days has been outstanding – thanks to those who have donated both en route and online. Also to everyone we have met, it helps us on our way.

A very wild, noisy night, constant roaring of trees and sea. Sunshine to greet us in in the morning which made us slow in getting off.

We were in holiday mood, and once away down hill, enjoyed coffee and croissants sitting outside a shop, fortified for the first uphill slog of the day. Lovely to see blue sky and blue greens of the sea and white rolling waves crashing on rocks at the base of cliffs.

From a sheltered vantage point had great view of seas, cliffs, and Wheal Coates mine chimney.

Wheal Coates Mine

Down to a car park, no pasties for sale, so off up again to cliff tops. It was extremely windy and hard to walk even with wind behind buffeting us along. At last we found a niche to eat a sarnie but no sketching as no view. St. Agnes headland was another 'corner' to turn, with all the headlands we'd walked disappearing behind us in mist. Ahead lay more dramatic coast.

We dropped steeply down to Trevanance bay, the waves rolling in looked tempting to sketch, but we wanted to find the campsite. So back on the path up and out of the hamlet, and once in phone signal, made a quick call to the campsite. A cheery voice answered, "we're open and the dog's fine".

Both felt tired of the wind and a little bad tempered. Glad to be welcomed on site by the owner. He showed us a sheltered spot by hedges, a nice place and very quiet – 1 camper, 1 tent. Good to have time to do a bit of washing and sort art stuff (getting very mucky) and clean self.

Need to get away earlier to get in earlier. Now cold and very windy. Barney full of life after a sleep. He seems ok with it all. We're settling in to tent routine though no more camp meals left.

Day 6 1/4 St Agnes to Newquay

Porth beach campsite	16.4miles
Fine, grey, wet in evening	2215 ft

A long day to get to the north side of Newquay. Again, superb coastline and strong westerly winds. Many painting opportunities for Jos but little time to make use of them.

Now we see the receding headlands behind us as we move up the coast – St Ives is now hardly in view away in the distance. Another noticeable change is in the stone walls – the picture shows the use of slate in a way we have never seen before, very sculptural

A detour inland is needed to cross a bridge over the river before Newquay, and then a steep hill to climb to the centre of town, hard work at the end of the day. Then it's Aldi and fish & chips.

After another mile or so we arrived at the Porthbeach Holiday Park just as it was getting dark. Once the staff saw us looking for a place to put up the tent we were soon sorted and to make a grand end to the day they donated £15.

Longest day yet, we got going by 10:30, back along cliff tops, the rock very red in colour. Not far along the cliffs, I got my phone out to take a photo when I noticed a message to ring Ben. Awful news, he told us our little 20 month old grandson in Australia, Archie, has a tumour and having tests done. He sounded upset and in shock, We felt stunned at the news, our poor family, so far away to help.

Taking in the news of Archie being diagnosed with a tumour

We carried on, both deep in thought, dropping down to Perranporth where a vast empty beach stretched ahead. We had coffee in a beach cafe full of dogs and sand. On the beach, we let Barney off to scamper about with the waves relentlessly piling in. At the end of the beach we rejoined the coast path and skirted round an old army camp.

Seeing some odd things on this walk

On to Holywells and more beach. Once over sand dune area, it was easy walking on grassy slopes. The rock changed to slate. At Pentre Point West, we had a good view up the entrance to the Gannel at high tide, with Newquay on its north bank.

Fascinating watching a skilled kite surfer skimming over the waves very fast

Then began a long, end of day, tiring section following the Gannel, through wood and over farmland. Finally we crossed it at a footbridge, then onto tarmac to reach Newquay. All dog tired, but Aldi and chippie loomed up. Fish & chips were very welcome. We still had a campsite to find, Porth Beach Tourist Park. Nearly dark when we arrived, wondering where to pitch. A friendly young man in a van showed us a sheltered spot. When he heard we were walking for charity, he wouldn't take £15. How generous people are.

18 miles and the dog is shattered, but we've got Newquay out of the way.

Still taking in this morning's news, we now wonder if the walk is on hold, will we have to stop, are we needed in Australia, family priorities, a worrying time. Nothing we can do now except wait for more news. Good to be in our tent, outside the wind is blowing and the sound of rain.

Day 7 2/4 Newquay to Porthcothan

Atlantic view campsite, Porthcothan	8.5 miles
Fine, then wet in night	1829 ft

A shorter day after the previous long one. We needed to stop early and recover. Not sure about sites so we took a chance on the first one and struck lucky. Most sites seem to be full of caravans with just small spaces (possibly) for backpackers but Atlantic View had about 20 acres of fields with just a few others pitched up and it was only £6 for all of us.
The wind has eased which makes for a more restful night.

A slow start as I made phone calls to Ben, Dan & Joanna. Ben very upset at the devastating news that Archie has cancer, it's not fair, poor little mite. Sal has arranged an appointment with a consultant for April 9th. She took Archie into A & E earlier this week with a severe nose bleed. Doctors started ball rolling, he was in for tests and this morning, our time, we learnt he has cancer, hard to believe. They have Easter weekend to get through and more tests next Tuesday to see if any more cancer in his little body. Then to Melbourne for treatment. The best outlook is removal of tumour and no spreading; the worst – must be spreading. Poor Dan & Sal, such a shock and worrying times ahead, one minute all is fine, next life changing. We said we'd go out when needed… so the whole walk may end, but meanwhile we carry on, as it's something to do and we can't do anything to help yet, as we would if we were nearer to them.

So with heavy hearts inside, we carried on coastal paths and yet more stunning cliffs, stacks and crashing waves. Mawgan Porth, Trenance Point, Carnewas.

A quick sketch and Barney makes the most of it

Carnewas Island

Just before Porthcothan we took a track to a campsite on a hill – Atlantic View. We needed an early stop. Very quiet fields and friendly man said £6 - £3 each! So we pitched in lee of a hedge and cooked our couscous, luckily bought in Aldi. Now dog and Bob flat out and I've had my Archers fix.

Barney's usual state on arrival at the days campsite

All very tired, one more day walking, then a rest at Keith's which we look forward to. A cloud now hangs over our journey, only a week in.

Card 1	Dear Jane,
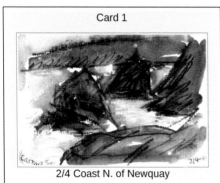

2/4 Coast N. of Newquay | We had v. sad news today from Oz. Our wee Archie has cancer, what was first thought a nasal polyp, turned to a malignant tumour. An op, chemo, plastic surgery in Melbourne next week after more tests after Easter. Such a shock for all the family. Ben v. upset on phone, also Dan.
We are carrying on walking until we hear more and whether they want us. All reeling. We've done 85 miles of stunning coast. The sea rolling in, relentlessly. Might ring you before you get this.
Lots Love
Jos, B & Brny |

Day 8 3/4 Porthcothan to Wadebridge

Easter break with cousin Keith	14.7 miles
Very windy	1266 ft

A day of strong winds along the coast and then wind and drizzle as we made our way along the Camel Trail from Padstow to Wadebridge.

First stop Porthcothan Village Store where Cornish pasties set us up for the 15 mile walk. Donations from both the shop owner and locals were much appreciated. We don't like making a thing of the charity collection with either campsite or shop owners – they have a steady stream of charity walkers and cyclists in this part of the world and can't give to everybody.

Padstow was busy with tourists as it was Good Friday. Jos managed a very quick water colour painting of the harbour – she never stops! Barney as usual was on the look out for food.

A near miss with another dog in the town centre which seemed to be attempting to attack every passing dog whilst the owner looked in shop windows.

Then onto the Camel Trail which was 5 miles of former railway line now hard surfaced which was uncomfortable at the end of the day. Many cyclists as cycle hire is available and well used. We saw 3 near misses with dog owners nearly having squashed pets as they failed to control the animals as cyclist passed.

Shortly before reaching Wadebridge we were met by cousin Keith, his wife Margaret and their golden retriever who were walking to meet us.

We are now staying with them for a day off – very welcome.

Our 39th wedding anniversary! Packed up after a good nights sleep; listening to rain. Managed to get off in 2 hours. Walked downhill to the village and stopped at friendly village shop for pasties, coffee and chat. More donations from owners. Off up coast and very windy again, having to concentrate to stay upright. At Treyarnon, after a wonderful pot of tea in the beach cafe, we headed east over track and footpath to Padstow. What a culture shock, a busy little town full of people, dogs, fudge and pasty shops.

We picnicked on a seat by the busy harbour packed with boats and I fitted today's sketch in:

Padstow Harbour

I passed so many sketching opportunities on this rugged coastline. After Padstow it was 5 miles of Camel way, a tarmac cycle track, way too hard for feet and muscles. Keith & Margaret met us and drove us back to their home in the village near Liskeard. They treated us to a Chinese takeaway, Bob & Keith chatting like true Mahons – non stop!

I wonder how little Archie and family are. Spoke to Tom on his houseboat and to Ben tonight who sounded more cheerful. Also rang friend Terri and that was good to share our news with another Grandma.

Day 9 4/4 Rest Day

A great day off. Cousin Keith and his wife Margaret gave us 5 star treatment with the added surprise of cousin Monica also turning up.

Easter Saturday.

Day off with Keith and Margaret. After lovely breakfast with us airing tent and hanging washing out, they took us on a drive round their 'patch'. We visited a menhir (a stone megalith), a stone circle and their son's house full of dogs and kids, then Liskeard and beach at Seaton on the calm south coast. - Phew.

Tretheny Quoit

Lovely sunny warm weather. A sunset as we enjoyed a roast lamb meal with other cousin Monica and husband. Great to have a family get together, lots of talking!

I phoned friends Rosie and Jane to share our sad news.

Day 10 5/4 Wadebridge to wild camp

Wild camp on Bounds Cliff past Port Isaac	8.8 miles
Sunny and warm	1319 ft

Keith dropped us off back at Wadebridge and we made our way to the coast at Port Isaac. Just had to have a Cornish cream tea. Then onto a wild camp on the coast path and wonderful views.

Easter Sunday.

Keith drove us back to Wadebridge. It was good to 'hit the trail' again on a nice still, warming up day, across fields to the lovely village of Chapel Amble where we sat outside an old pub for orange and soda. Later, lunch by a stream where I heard chiff-chaff calling, first avian sign of spring.

Enjoyed following the route through copses, muddy fields and one cow field (sleepy cows, phew), passing an old church on our way.

Narrow street in Port Isaac

On arrival at Port Isaac, there was a very steep descent down a narrow road of old cottages to the harbour where usual fudge shop and pub with ½ covered outdoor seating.

Our first Cornish cream tea

We had a 6 cup pot of tea and our first Cornish cream tea of scones, jam and clotted cream – Very good.

Set off for cliffs in sun and blue sky – hooray!

When we came to a running stream, we decided to pitch the tent – bit rough and uneven but a good call, I had time to paint headlands before tea and listen to the Archers.

Lovely pink sky, Joanna rang, she sounded OK.

Tresungers Point

9:10pm sound of running water, time to read and reflect, mixed feelings. As we left Wadebridge, we passed a charity shop window, a poster 'Short Precious Lives' caught my eye and I thought of little Archie. Then I enjoyed being in the moment, the birds, landscape, sea – the future for him unknown. Other elements are so constant, the tides, the cycle of the year, spring – the feel of renewal, summer migrants returning, yet… what's going to happen to him? We have to wait.

Camping

Typical wild camp near a stream

Our camping is based on tried and tested equipment and routines. For the trek, we used a Hilleberg Kaitum 2 tent which had served us well for 5 years on many backpacking trips in the Scottish Highlands. Choice of tent is always based on compromises. The Kaitum is big enough to include two humans and a large dog along with space for all our belongings regardless of the weather, yet light enough to carry when backpacking long distances. The tunnel structure offers plenty of space for the size yet is stable (although noisy) in strong winds. Lightweight titanium pegs helped keep the weight down and we also carried a couple of large plastic pegs, for use on the two main end guy-lines which are useful in sandy conditions.

The tent has two porches, one at each end which meant we could safely cook whilst offering a way out for Barney when required. Porches also served as storage and drying areas. They have substantial ventilation sections which help to keep condensation down when the porches and doors are fully closed.

Both wind and midges can be major problems when camping in Scotland so doors with mesh screens (to stop midges) that can be completely covered (to stop the wind) and yet can offer adequate ventilation (when it's hot) is important. The Kaitum has plenty of flexibility with fully opening doors and porches. This is particularly useful when Jos wants to paint but outdoor conditions such as rain or midges otherwise prevent it.

We use a specially made, lightweight 'footprint' to protect the tent floor. A tent footprint goes under the tent to protect the waterproof floor from damage. Also, we use another layer of material to protect the tent floor from the dog's paws which was placed under his bed. It was also spread over the end of our sleeping bags to stop them getting wet or dirty from mucky paws.

We both have high quality sleeping bags with silk liners and inflatable mattresses. The mattresses are inflated by a battery powered pump – a small luxury well worth carrying when having to blow up two mattresses every day for months. Barney has a piece of insulating foam which he is quite happy to sleep on in the 'space' at the end of Jos's feet.

Day 11 6/4 Cliff wild camp to Trethevey

Trewethett Farm Caravan Club Site past Tintagel	9.8 miles
Very clear and sunny, hot	3298 ft

> *The coast is superb and now the wind has dropped and the sun is shining. This however makes for hard work as the coast path is as hard as all the guide books say, with continuous ups and downs. A day of walking easily matches a mountain day out. Tent finally up on a plush site.*

Easter Monday.

Cold night. Bright blue skies all day, first time wearing shorts.

One of the many descents on the South West Coast Path

Lovely route, steeply up and down many headlands. The sea turquoise blue, no wind and all very tranquil until we dropped down to Trebarwith where there were masses of people!

We got a seat at a cafe and had pasties but Bob was very unrelaxed, with all the dogs and crying children... Peace when we left and headed for cliffs until

49

Tintagel, then more masses. But we skirted round the 'castle' and enjoyed more dramatic cliffs and sea.

Willapark Headland, Lye Rock and The Sisters from Trethevey

Getting tired now, just a few more very steep up and down steps – Rocky Valley with a campsite temptingly above. Very friendly man – "pitch anywhere you like", we pitched at the cliff edge facing Willapark headland. Lye Rock, the Sisters, Bossiney Haven, dark shapes against a fiery low setting sun. I tried painting it.

Painting the sunset

Lovely to have tea outside the tent in sun. Bob seems tired. As I write, all I can hear is the sound of waves, cry of gulls, some tawny owls and campers bedding down – very peaceful. I wonder how they are in Oz 7:30am there, we'll find out in the morning.

Day 12 7/4 Trethevey to Crackington Haven

Camp on café lawn	9 miles
Hot, sunny until sea fog at 5pm	2821 ft

Hard day which included the highest cliff in Cornwall called... High Cliff! Met up with a walking party from Milton Keynes – Hi all. Boscastle stop for an ice cream, very touristy.
We were going to wild camp but the kind owner of the Cabin Cafe offered us the use of her garden – thanks a lot. That meant we had a pub meal and wifi.

Woke early worrying and wondering about Archie results but didn't get any message. We recharged phones in site shop, £20 campsite fee as it's Caravan Club, but enjoyed lovely hot showers and great facilities.

Set off 10ish, soon in shorts, blue skies and HOT! A long day of yet more steep ups and downs.

As we neared Boscastle, the place severely flooded in 2004, the path was above a narrow harbour, cafes lined the river and we stopped for lovely ice cream. While Bob & Barney sat in the shade, I found the Spar for provisions.

180° view of Boscastle harbour

Then began a lot of steep steps up and steep back down as we went up one headland after another. Beeny, Rusey to High Cliff (highest in Cornwall) with great views of 'longshore drift' - the series of waves coming in to vast Strangles Beach.

A walking group stopped for lunch with Barney watching intently

I had to stop and paint from the cliff.

After all the steep ascents and descents today, we grew very tired and my right upper ankle hurting (hope not shin splints).

Cambeak from the High Cliff

At last made it to Crackington Haven, by this time an eerie thick sea fog had descended and we could hardly see the sea, only hear the waves below.

I'm glad we stopped at the Cabin Cafe with its smoky log burners outside. We had a huge pot of tea with scones and cream to set us up for hiking up cliffs to seek a wild camp. The kind cafe lady said "Use my lawn."

Cabin Cafe lawn – perhaps one of our more unusual campsites

So here we are, pitched on a fenced in flat lawn, with sound of sea and just had a good pub meal and pint of Doom Bar. Spent evening on our phones, Bob blogging and me talking to Ben & Jo. Archie has a rare cancer, Rhabdomyosarcoma. Results of tests come tomorrow, what a nightmare for them, we are so far away, carrying on, but nothing else we can do, so on we go.

Just so much coast I could be painting, but we are getting a taste and feel of the coast path, definitely return for more, as long as my foot is ok.

Day 13 8/4 Crackington Haven to Menachurch Point

Dunsmouth Farm wild camp past Bude	12.5 miles
Hot, sunny	2588 ft

Hard walking at first then a real holiday beach. Restocking at Sainsburys as we have another hard section to come...

Sunny, pleasant start. Coffee x 2 and bacon baps at Cabin Cafe. Charged phones and got message that Archie has no spread, they sounded very positive and away to Melbourne for treatment.

Another 'down' with a view of the next 'up'

We set off in cheerful mood, up and down steps, the gradient gradually easing off at Millock, where the path went through oak woods at the back of the cliffs. All very geologically interesting, strata visible on the shore too. Such a contrast, when we looked down on Widemouth Bay, a seaside beach full of holiday makers.

Widemouth Sand

We stopped for our picnic, got signal and found Ben had more worrying news about Archie, more tests, might be cancer with not good prognosis, Dan worried, poor son and Sal. What can we do?

We walked on and met a family from Bideford who made a big fuss of Barney and said they'd put their address up on the blog if we want to call by. Another local man told us of a farm field with a portaloo up the coast and to take our time so we see the beauty of the area, also informed us where Sainsburys is in Bude.

Holiday atmosphere in Bude

So instead of camping on a site south of Bude as 'planned' we plodded on into Bude and out to Sainsburys on the edge of town where I resupplied us with food. Then off along coast path again, up more steep steps hoping we'd find a good place for the night. Fortunately (as Bob tired and very grumpy) we arrived at said farmers field with water on tap, a portaloo, a few other tents and sun just setting, so up with tent and soon a meal cooking. Now it's 10pm, sea thundering below, cliffs very crumbling and not very far away. Just texted Dan, such a shame all the worry they face – wonder when we should go over?

Day 14 9/4 Wild camp on cliffs to Hartland Quay

Stoke Barton campsite on hill above Hartland Quay	12.9 miles
Very hot. Sunny	4211 ft

A hard day. The SWCP (South West Coast Path) isn't easy – this day had ascent the same as Ben Nevis and it was too hot!
On one climb, Barney stepped over an adder on the path, luckily unhurt.
Arrived exhausted but no dogs allowed in the hotel, where we wondered if we could camp, so a steep walk up to a campsite. However, kind people gave us a lift – thanks. We're hoping to meet up for a pint when we get to Monmouth.
Also today, we left Cornwall and entered Devon.

Cold clear starry night. I got up at 6:30 and saw the sunrise over fields, then it began to warm up as a very nippy start, but what a day it turned into:

It was so hot for walking cliffs to Hartland Quay, well, backpacking with all the steep descents into stream valleys and steep ascents (over 4000ft). Very hard work the last 4 miles with a sore back, but stunning coastline all day, although not much time to linger and take it in.

We passed Morwenstow but didn't go to look at the Norman church.

A vicar, Rev. Hooker, built a hut from driftwood and it's still there tucked into the cliffs. Then it was into Devon – our first County boundary.

2 weeks into the trek and we finally leave Cornwall

So relieved to reach the hotel at Hartland Quay as sun setting over sea, but no camping and no dogs in hotel. Luckily a man overheard and said he and his wife going to a campsite uphill, and we could have a lift. Long chat with them – from Monmouth, so may see them later.

Had good chats with people on the path, handing out cards.

Poor Barney, so hot for him today, he's snoring now. A very strenuous day.

We didn't get news from Oz today, phones now on charge at the site house.

Near Hartland Quay

Day 15 10/4 Hartland Quay to Clovelly

The Red Lion, Clovelly	11.1 miles
	3187

A switchback start took us to 'the turn' and we started walking east rather than north.
Flatcoat owners Grace & Izzie were without their dog so Barney got lots of attention.
A steadier walk eventually led to Clovelly where we met up with Neil from Guide Dogs for a publicity shoot. Then we found the Red Lion Hotel on the quayside had a dog friendly room so we took it. What a room, old and overlooking the harbour – very special. A good meal, live music and we did all our washing.

Up at 7am, still tired after our long hot day and late camp meal (Uncle Ben's rice). Nice morning, fresher. A very friendly girl running site and shop was most concerned re. Archie. She and her mum loved Barney. We had our phones charged up in their house, so had good chat with Dan & Ben. Dan said more tests needed to find out what sort of cancer, whether aggressive type or not, then decision next Wednesday regarding treatment. Good X-Ray results showed cancer not in bone structure of nose. Archie 'talked' to me on the phone! Hard to believe it's all happening to them, we 'forget' as we walk and enjoy the scenery, the rugged coast, cliffs and lovely primroses, bluebells. Just today, all sorts of flowers and lots of birdsong especially in the woods, then we remember the hard times our children are having.

Today wasn't as hard, a few steep ups and downs to Hartland point lighthouse and coffee kiosk.

Blackchurch Rock

Then flat fields, hedgerows, a big drop to a stream valley, woodland and pasture before a steep road down to Clovelly. All cobbled narrow steep streets. Met Neil from Guide Dogs South West who took photos of us – poor man had 2 new hips and awaiting knee op!

Up the steps to the room at the Red Lion Hotel, Clovelly

Bob found us a room at the hotel on the quay, an odd shaped corner room looking out over the harbour. Lovely to shower, wash clothes, have good meal in pub and meet locals along with a singer Talulah who'd been to Hexham and maybe our local pub, the Crown in Catton. Bedtime in comfy bed now.

Very characterful room and place – a real treat too.

Card 2 10/4 Blackchurch Rock from Windbury Point  on the way to Clovelly (Posted 15/4 Post Box at Challacombe)	Dear Jane, Thinking of you as we walk now in Devon 'on the edge' with rugged cliffs on our left & red brown earth ploughed fields on our right – Bude to Hartland Point was tough in the heat with all the ups & downs. Barney plodding along well, always glad to rest!! Archie on our minds now awaiting more test results to learn how aggressive the cancer is – he 'talked' to me on my mobile this morn!! What a shame. Archie's Story is on Facebook apparently. Love Jos xx

Day 16 11/4 Clovelly to near Bideford

Greencliff farm 'hideaway' campsite, Abbotsham	10.3 miles
Sunny, cooler	3389 ft

A fine start to the day with a full English breakfast. Then a pleasant woodland walk following the coast for a few miles. More ups and downs (they always come together!) to reach a lovely little campsite at Greencliff Farm, west of Bideford. The site owner's son kindly did some shopping for us so we are staying 2 nights to have a rest day.

The day started with cups of tea in bed and hotel breakfast including bacon, sausage and egg – very filling.

A quiet Clovelly

Back up the steep cobbled street, still quiet as earlyish, then walk began, easy start contouring round in woodland and fields, lovely to hear birds singing. Saw a blackcap, such a melodic song, if we had a chance to sit still, might have seen lots. Loads of chiff-chaff calling.

Walking got harder as we had stream valleys to drop down to and climb back up. Even reached sea level at one point. My heels are both blistering, so boots must be rubbing, not usual for me to have to use Compeed, I hope it's not a problem. Nearly reached the end of our coastal walking when we get to Barnstable. We turned up at a very quiet C&C* site on a farm, Greencliff only 10 minutes from cliffs. Very friendly woman Sarah showed us the lawn and facilities then came back to take a shopping list as her son was going down to Westward Ho! We do meet some nice people.

Today Barney attracted attention and we gave cards out – it's all adding up.

Day 17 12/4 Rest Day camped at Greencliff farm.

12 paintings!

> *A day off. Barney has slept all day, Bob has been reading a book and Jos has produced 12 paintings down at the shore.*
> *This our last night at the coast, tomorrow we head inland to Exmoor.*
> *Note: Please feel free to comment directly on blog posts – we're never quite sure anybody's reading this stuff. (many comments on the blog after this post telling us people were following it).*
> *I thought I should post a few notes about our posts. If you don't see anything for a few days it's not because we've got a problem. We need 2 things to post from my phone – a connection (phone or wifi) and some power remaining in the phone battery. Quite often we have no connection.*
> *One difficulty we have is keeping the phones charged. Often we go 3 or 4 days between recharges, so you get a flurry of posts as we try to catch up before going to bed.*
> *We have a fuel cell USB charger with us but it only worked once before packing in.*
> *I have found I can get a days entry in whilst Jos is painting, now we have a phone signal.*
> *It's 9pm so time for bed (Barney's been asleep for ages). Night night.*

Just been to the farmhouse to recharge, Sarah said she lived in Ponteland as a child and stayed at Deneholme† with school.

Sun and wind, wind getting up, blowing tent. Phone calls to Joanna, spoke to Tom & Ben, all there. So nice to hear –our close family.

Barney slept all day and Bob reading while I painted.

Good to have a rest day, our first really on our own, me sorting out sketches, when and where done en route. Dog catching up on sleep.

* Camping and Caravanning Club
† Deneholme is an outdoor centre in our local village of Allendale.

North of Greencliff

Just enjoyed a few hours by myself painting from Greencliffs. Interesting with sweep of grey pebble beach, rocks in line going out horizontally and cliffs overhanging and falling. Behind, the lush green grass, hedged Devon farmland, a real contrast at the edge – silver light, grey sea, hard to catch with skill. Good to use 12 sheets of paper.

Some of the days paintings

Day 18 13/4 Greencliff farm to Barnstaple

Brightlycott Farm Campsite past Barnstaple	19.9 miles
Hot!	1581 ft

The last day of section 1 of the walk, more accurately titled Before Bideford to after Barnstaple.

After the very last mile of coast to Westward Ho! we turned inland! Done it at last – including Westward Ho! in the sentence means it has 2 exclamation marks! (done it again!) I believe Westward Ho! is the only place name in the UK to include one but no doubt somebody will tell me that's wrong!

Andy Robinson's short cut to Bideford was easy to follow and we were soon having coffee in a bistro. Then came the old railway line to Barnstaple – 9 miles of tarmac cycle track in the heat. We all found it uncomfortable and when Barney started to slow I went on ahead to make sure I got to Barnstaple before the shops shut. Mistake – I began to sense the reoccurrence of a blister on the ball of one foot but Jos had the Compeeds.

By the time we got to the campsite in the evening we both had multiple blisters – we all hate road walking!

As I also developed an ankle problem we have decided to take another rest day here and recover. Barney is happy about that.

Phew a very long hot day. Started early – up at 6:30am and away by 8:35

Packing up. Barney sits some distance away when he doesn't want to be loaded up

It was a lovely, peaceful site at £14 per night. Back to the coast to walk fairly gently towards Westward Ho! Then following our man's notes, we went on field footpaths wending our way to Bideford. Met a man with a collie on the cliffs who was interested in Barney's Ruffwear bags and later a woman with a huge Schnauzer also wanting same. Gave them and a spaniel owner our cards.

The River Torridge, Bideford

Found a dog friendly cafe and enjoyed good coffee x 2 and gave cards to the girls. It felt a milestone reached on crossing the long bridge over the Torridge. Back on the coast path, an ex railway line, now TARMAC cycle-path, we suffered in the heat.

Such a drag with long straight stretches, bikes merrily passing both ways. Loads of birds in trees and bushes lining the sides, reed bunting, willow warblers and saw egrets in marshes.

Bob 'shot off' to make sure he got to Millets for gas, but in doing so, he has hurt his ankle, which may mean another rest day tomorrow.

Barney and I took it slowly, resting in the shade, bird watching and having a pot of tea and ice cream at Fremington station. We met up again at Barnstaple where Bob had Co-op shopped as well as Millets and Boots. His ankle pain started after we had a pint of orange outside a pub. Then a long hike out of town and steep uphill to the farm campsite. We were hailed by a young woman as we rested by a petrol station (Bob putting Compeed on). She's (Sophia) intending to do the Appalachian Trail next year and wanted to pick our brains re backpacking. Later she brought us fresh made flapjacks to the tent, how kind.

Hot and sunny the next morning, Barney finding shade

So finally after 21 long hot miles, we are in the tent, dosing on ibuprofen. Down below are the orange lights of Barnstaple, sound of traffic and planes. Also barn and tawny owl. Bedtime.

Day 19 14/4 Rest Day

It's ironic that after all the ups and downs of the coast path (and there were many of them), we find the completely flat section the hardest. Barney is appreciating another rest however.
It was a hard climb to get up here at the end of yesterday, Jos listened to the Archers on our tiny radio on the way up the steep part.

Section 2. The Bristol Channel and the Welsh borders

Barnstaple to Knighton

2 nights with relatives, 8 with friends, 3 pub, 2 wild camp and 10 campsites	219.5 miles
More like a British spring.	26914 ft

After the stunning coastline of the South West Coast Path, stage 2 of our walk took us across Exmoor and the hills of North Somerset, on to the flat lands of the Somerset levels then the dramatic Cheddar Gorge. Next, Bristol and over the Bristol Channel to the Welsh Border where we followed the Offa's Dyke trail for several days as far as Knighton.

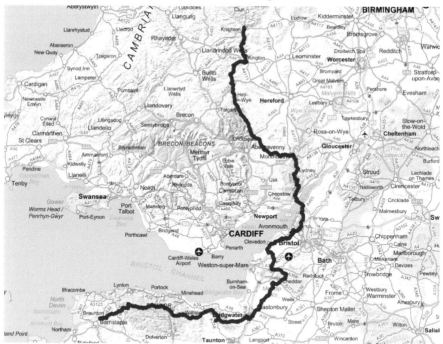

Now we are leaving the South West Coastal Path to head inland, making for the ranges of hills that overlook the Bristol Channel, ridges we had never walked on, the highest points on Exmoor, and the Brendon and Quantock hills.

Exmoor Sunset

Wonderful high level walking with views across to the Welsh hills and coast.

After descending to Bridgwater to cross the River Parrett, we walked the flat, Fen like Somerset Levels where we had to run from inquisitive herds of cows and bull, once cutting a knotted binder twine bound gate in our escape!

Horse & Cheddar

On to Cheddar and the famous gorge which we climbed up before arriving at another range of hills, the Mendips. Our destination, Bristol, (to stay with a friend and pick up parcel of sketchbooks etc.) reached by disused railway / cycle tracks, and little used footpaths often close to the out of sight M5 motorway. It felt a big milestone to reach the M5 bridge crossing the river Avon.

We were amazed how the guide book took us around Bristol by a series of low wooded ridges, our route avoiding the urban sprawl. We made our way to the muddy shores of the River Severn by more little used paths through fields (more cow avoidance), crossing the Severn by an interminably long road bridge, the M48, to enter Wales at Chepstow.

Offa's Dyke National Trail

From here, we followed the Offa's Dyke path, a national trail, northwards to Knighton on the Shropshire border. This took us through pastoral, lush, green, hilly farmland, and woods full of bluebells along with airy walking on whale-back ridges near to the Black mountains. We passed through the small towns of Monmouth, Hay on Wye and Kington. This stage took 18 days including 2 rest days at Monmouth and Pandy. We also had an additional 6 day 'blister break ' an unforeseen and very welcome stop with kind friends off-route in Dorset (after hobbling off Exmoor).*

It rained every day whilst in Wales. No wonder it was so green and lush.

Day 20 15/4 Barnstaple to Pinkery pond on Exmoor

Wild camp on Exmoor	14 miles
Hot day, breezy in night	2724 ft

Our (Bob & Jos) feet are put to the test.
Lovely woodland walk followed by steady uphill to get onto Exmoor. Another very hot day with full sunshine.

What a long and another hot day, both suffering with our blisters, Bob only just managed to get here, bit sad seeing him struggling with pain behind me. Started off ok, my heels felt sore on roads after we left the farm, but better in the woodland. Enjoyed the shade, scents and birdsong (before that we had an

* Blame that Barnstaple hot cycle track.

unpleasant mile on a busy road not long after leaving the farm). Came out of woods at Loxhore Mill and then more road walking up and up to Bratton Fleming where it was good to find a shop for ice cream, drink, bread, cake and more paracetamol.

Drying the tent while resting in the shade

Then as it was midday – it was very HOT, more road walking and fast cars, Barney by now ready to flop, so we had a good break in the shade of a hedge on a minor road.

After that we had Challacombe village to aim for and it was back on rough bridle path down and up on uneven ground that made Bob miserable with his sore feet. Mine hurting too – perhaps I can bear pain more? That's women for you, more used to it! When we reached a farm at the top of a hill, I took our water bottles and the farmer's wife filled them up for us.

Packhorse (Packdog?) bridge, Challacombe

We had a break by a picturesque stream and packhorse bridge before setting off up a bridle track for the moors. This is where Bob started lagging behind, as I pushed ahead, enjoying being back on hills and open space. Still a long hike to Woodbarrow (a round circular mound), where we could see other hill tops, even across to S. Wales. Eventually we reached Pinkery Pond, our wild camp for the night. I put the tent up while Bob filtered water – I even cooked the tea! He is in a bad way but ate tea and now we are ready to zonk out. Only wish we had news from Dan. Just a message from Ben that they are still waiting tests – 2 weeks now. I wonder what is going to happen…. All quiet here, 2 Canada geese calling from the pond.

Day 21 16/4 Pinkery pond to Hillhead Cross

Wild camp on edge of Exmoor in stubble field above Exford	9.2 miles
Cool start, hot. Lovely warm evening	676 ft

Camped in a field above Exford. Great trouble finding water today although we're not far from the river Ex.
We're making slow and sometimes painful progress across Exmoor.

Pinkery Pond

Did a couple of paintings of the quiet pond while Bob took the tent down and off we went. He's more cheerful with the soft, grassy, but uneven going. Exmoor is all dry, white long grass, not heathery. I chatted to a man on the other side of a fence who was surveying ancient monuments, barrows (mounds / tombs). He had a job on.

Bob's feet and ankle got worse and at one time he tried walking in socks. I took the tent and gas but couldn't for long as the extra weight made my hip hurt. What a pair! We had a bit of a problem finding the route. I went ahead and sussed out a path through a sheep field. We dropped down the 'Postman's Path' to Warren Mill Farm which Bob had heard of so much in his planning as a place to stay. I knocked at the door to ask for water to refill our bottles. Then off uphill on a very rough bridle track. By now we needed to find water so we could camp. We had noticed a stream on the map but when we reached it, it was surrounded by electric fence!

I thought I'd ask at the 'big house' on whose land it was, but a large 'Beware of Dog' sign at the road end put me off. I didn't want my ankles bitten by a guard dog. Instead I climbed over a high fence and hedge into a field where I'd spotted a tractor working and flagged it down. A somewhat surprised young man, very tanned, with a strong Somerset accent, told me that Ranolph Fiennes lived there. He didn't think Ranolph was at home as he was in the desert.[*] He suggested we could call for water at houses further along

[*] Sir Ranolph Fiennes, the British explorer, was taking part in the gruelling desert race Marathon des Sables, raising money for the cancer charity Marie Curie.

the road. We started walking, very tired by now then lo and behold found a trickle of water flowing out of a culvert under the road. Relieved, Bob began filtering and we found a stubble field nearby to pitch, Phew.

Here we are, both with throbbing feet and a glorious Exmoor sunset to paint.

Exmoor Sunset

Day 22 17/4 Exmoor to Luxborough

The Royal Oak Inn, Luxborough.	11.7 miles
Cool on Dunkery Beacon, shower of rain, nice and warm at Luxborough	1324 ft

Dunkery Beacon and Barney gets his share of the jelly babies! A habit we got into whilst doing Munros in Scotland.
Dunkery Beacon isn't quite 3000ft but Barney knows it's the top. Next was pleasant woodland walking and oh, nearly forgot, we're in Somerset. Made our way slowly to Luxborough and a room in the pub – wonderful!

We descended from the hills via Dunkery Beacon thinking we were coming down into Hobbiton with green, lush fields, pigs, (orcs?) and beautiful cattle in barns. Entering Luxborough we passed thatched cottages, grass being strimmed, old people wandering about with garden compost in wheelbarrows. On arrival at the Inn, Douglas, a very friendly young man welcomed us in.

Heading down to Hobbiton

This morning we packed up from our 'private' field after ringing Dan in Oz. He and family were just away out of the hospital with the good news that Archie has the 'better' type of cancer i.e. not so aggressive. Chemo starts tomorrow and continues for 12 weeks.

What a time they are having, wish we could help out, still can, wait till things 'sort' out and see. Meanwhile, so good to get positive news.

Somerset Fields – approaching Luxborough

We just enjoyed cider (me), beer (Bob) and a lovely meal at the Royal Oak Inn. Lovely friendly service. Chatted to a couple who know Papworth, my childhood home and they also raise funds for Guide Dogs.

And here we are, Bob soaking in a BATH, me on the bed in a cosy little room at the front, with a stream under the window. What luxury to be had.

Card 3	Dear Jane,
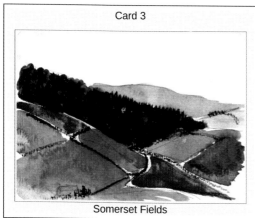 Somerset Fields	Somerset fields are very green or brown. We camped on Exmoor at Pinkery Pond, then in a stubble field getting water from a culvert. Walking off Dunkery Beacon to Luxbrough a hamlet like Hobbiton, very lush, thatched roofs & good pub / Inn where we stayed. Archie news more positive thank goodness. Treatment underway now so got to go thro' chemo etc. We resting up at Penny & Tims in Charmouth b4 next leg to Quantocks, Bristol...xx

On hold

We are taking a few days off in order to give our (Bob & Jos) blisters a better chance of healing. Continued walking is slowly making matters worse and we are getting slower.

Barney's feet are holding up fine. Jos applies Mushers cream daily which is keeping his pads soft – perhaps that's what we need.

Our old friends Penny & Tim* have kindly offered to pick us up Saturday so we can spend some time with them at their home in Dorset. We'll be back on the route as soon as we can.

Up to now, Barney has walked 238 miles and collected over £1000 for Guide Dogs

Stay tuned.

* Penny & Tim were neighbours in Northumberland when our children were young.

The dread of all long distance walkers, blisters are normally avoidable. Unfortunately, circumstance meant we (Jos & Bob that is, not Barney) incurred them after the long hot tramp along the tarmac surfaced Tarka Trail on Day 18. We had no alternative footwear to our lightweight walking boots and socks which meant over-hot feet and an inevitable outcome.

We were planning on meeting up with old friends from Northumberland now living in Dorset. Originally for them to accompany us for a stage but once they heard of our predicament, Penny & Tim suggested they put us up while we recovered, a wonderful, generous offer which we took up.

Day 23 18/4 Off to Sunny Dorset

Lovely morning. Packed after inn breakfast and sat in sun waiting for Tim & Penny. They hadn't changed! We were all chatting away in the car as they drove us back to Dorset via Axminster to shop for Compeed etc.

So lucky for us, here we are at their lovely airy house with sea views, resting and healing our bloody blisters. P, T and I had a walk (5 mins) to the sea and across a bridge over the river to the caravan site where I stayed for holidays with Mum and Dad, it's still there but more modern. Barney very happy to run round with no sacks to carry.

Charmouth

Eventually we stayed with them for 6 days whilst wounds healed and we enjoyed a holiday by the sea.

Days 24 – 28 19/4 – 23/4

A few notes I made during our 'holiday'...

Restful SUNNY day here! Bob staying put, Penny, Tim and I walk on beach – lots of chat, lots to catch up on.

P and I walked up the coast, their friends joined us for a good walk up the hill opposite. Bob's feet ok, mine too.

My new Keen sandals 6 ½ arrived and are a good fit. Packed things, day went.

Golden Cap Cliffs

Bob & I shopped for bread and supplies. In the evening, we all went to Lyme Regis for a meal together in lovely restaurant with good fish and veggie selection. A big thank-you for P & T, great we were all so relaxed in each others company.

Relaxing with Penny

Penny and I caught the bus (using our OAP bus cards) to Lyme Regis to walk on the Cob – the curling harbour wall, and see the town. I bought books for Thierry & Geordie and a bee for Archie. He has begun chemo now, poor little mite, but it's for the good, so see how it all works out and whether we can help in their comings and goings.

Day 29 24/4 Luxborough to Monksilver

The Notley Arms, Monksilver	7.6 miles
Warm, close, humid	1152 ft

> ### Back to it!
>
> *First, our thanks to Penny & Tim for helping us out over the last week. We had a wonderful time with them in Charmouth while our wounds healed and we were able to get stuff posted to us easily. This morning they took us back to Luxborough where they had picked us up nearly a week ago.*
>
> *Today's walk has brought us to the edge of Exmoor at Monksilver – a good country walk.*
>
> *We're staying at the pub tonight so it's time for a shower before food.*

4 weeks since we started walking. So 3 weeks on, 1 week off. 3 weeks and 237 miles to get to Luxborough.

WALKING AGAIN!

The Luxborough Inn, The Royal Oak

We said our goodbyes back at Luxborough. Then began an undulating walk, often on ways - 'hollow ways', sunken lanes between walls and undergrowth, like walking through a tunnel. We met up with a very friendly farmer who is holidaying in Northumberland this year!

It became hot for the uphills and green valleys. We could see the distant line of the Quantocks. No curlews or lapwings yet.

Very friendly bar / owner at the Notley Inn, Monksilver. Now I'm falling asleep after a lush, tasty meal.

Day 29 update

I felt I must post an addendum to today's post.

We have just had a lovely meal in the Notley Arms Inn at Monksilver and after talking to the local people at the next table were given £40 for Barney's collection – thanks. We've been amazed at the generosity of people we have met on the walk – thanks to all who have donated so far.

Have also just had contact with Kay & Nigel who saw us off from Land's End nearly a month ago. Kay told us just how important her guide dog is to her and how her life was transformed by the help her dog gives. Every donation helps people like Kay – every donation is appreciated.

Forgot to say in last post about the map. Jos carries the days printed map pages in a plastic case. Unfortunately her trouser pockets are not very deep and it has fallen out several times. (Women's outdoor trousers have useless pockets she says). Up to now I have been behind and picked it up but not this time, we soon realised it was missing. However, a while later a knock at the door and the landlord presented it to us! A local person had found it on the path and seeing the pub telephone number, delivered it. Many thanks!

Day 30 25/4 Monksilver to Goathurst

Huntstile Organic farm	14.5 miles
Cloudy, good for walking, heavy rain 4pm on. Roads became rivers.	2043 ft

Quantocks day.

First a crossing of the West Somerset railway and a steam train. Then up onto the ridge with ponies and trig points.

Late afternoon and the weather changed with our first day time rain for weeks. Very wet and some very difficult stiles to negotiate.

Arriving at Enmore we tried the pub but weren't even allowed in with the dog. A phone call to Huntstile Organic Farm to confirm camping and they offered to pick us up. Soon drying out and then the offer of a meal which was gladly accepted. Lizzie and John gave us a room (donated to Barney's mission) – very generous and many thanks! The house and the room could take pages to describe – take a look at www.huntstileorganicfarm.co.uk to see why we were blown away by both the place and the people.

If you're ever in this part of the country, do visit-it's not to be missed.

What a place we are in this evening, a panelled room dating back to 1430 with a massive double bed and bathroom the size of our front room!

To work backwards, very wet and tired, after a long day we reached Enmore. We walked into the pub with wet dog – NO dogs and no room. So we very luckily made a call to this place that Bob found which did camping. Liz said I'll come and pick you up! A soft spoken man, John, soon arrived and drove us to their farm (Huntstile Organic) and invited us in for a hot drink. After much friendly chatting, we were invited to have supper with them, pork stroganoff from home-grown pork. Such an interesting old place and so friendly people. 2 'woofers' (Willing Workers on Organic Farms) were also at the farm table, a young Sicilian girl Johanna and Peter, a Yorkshireman. Barney was fussed over, fed and dried out in front of the stove. When we asked where to pitch the tent, Liz & John kindly decided to give us a room for the night as 'donation' to the walk – what generosity – can't wait to see the place in daylight.

Going back to this morning, after a lovely breakfast and warm goodbyes in the very hospitable Notley Arms, off we went up hill, along edges of fields, over and under stiles, past very posh homes and across a railway line where we saw a real steam train puffing by.

West Somerset Railway

It took 2 hours to walk 3 miles to Bicknoller where three kind old ladies told us the village community shop did tea, run by a bearded, aproned gentleman, just like in the Archers, with villagers volunteering.

After tea and cake in the warm, we took a sandy, wooded track up to the Quantocks. We enjoyed a good hike with distant views of the Bristol Channel, Wales, and back to Dunkery Beacon, Exmoor.

Quantock Hills looking west

We had a picnic at a trig. point[*] where I painted and rain began to patter as we left the hills. We began the long next stage alongside ploughed fields, over and under tricky stiles, heavy rain by now. It was getting dark by the time we dripped into the unfriendly pub at Enmore, when such a surprise began to unfold.

Day 31 26/4 Huntstile Farm to Bawdrip

Staying with friends at Middlezoy	9.4 miles
Cloudy cool start after rain to blue skies especially end of day	223 ft

Onto the Somerset Levels and heading for Bridgwater after our stay at Huntstile. Some of the stiles have been difficult, the picture below shows a collapsed bridge we had to get over.

Found Morrisons and met up with Sheila's[†] niece Emma, her husband Richard and daughter Grace. They kindly offered to put us up after we finished the days walk and took our bags so we travelled light. Barney was very pleased (and us).

Cows are now a problem – we had to re route rapidly at one point.

After Richard and Grace picked us up we were taken on a tour of the levels around their village, the whole area was affected by the floods and we saw the bridge which featured on the tv reports.

Another lovely evening, we're being spoiled!

* Trigonometrical (or triangulation) point used for surveying and mapping.
† Sheila is Jos's sister-in-law.

A relaxed start today, waking up in a soft enormous bed! We had dried everything out on radiators in the huge bathroom, in daylight we saw where we were, a fascinating old house with large veg. gardens, chalets, caravans, all very well kept. We were invited into a dining room for breakfast with Liz & John and 2 guests. I chose tasty muesli and all on the house – such generosity.

Missing bridge

Took a while to sort out and pack before leaving to start walking to Bridgwater over **level** fields – very pleasant. Bob carried Barney's bags and it is good to see him romping about, rolling and being a dog. In the town, after all the meadows, we found a Morrisons for the usual. Emma, Richard & Grace came out from Middlezoy on the levels to meet us. They kindly offered a bed and even took our bags so we were free to walk without weight. Great, as quite a bit of streets and alleyways to walk on to get out of Bridgwater and into open countryside. We crossed the noisy M5 on a pedestrian bridge, what a contrast to the quiet Somerset lanes.

After a good hike on a track between two drains like in the Fens, we found we had cow problems with the footpath going straight through bull, cow and calf fields, no thank you.

Don't mix with these when walking with a dog

In one field we had to run to a gate before the herd got to us and then similar with another herd. Too close for comfort and so good not carrying sacks. Glad to reach the road.

Richard picked us up to take us to their lovely home in Middlezoy village and showed us the River Parrot and its shoring up after the floods. Very Fen like (reminds me of the flat landscape of the Cambridgeshire Fens where Grandma lived).

Lovely evening meal with Emma, Richard and Grace and seeing how Barney got on with their 2 dogs. He was actually dominated by the younger dog!

Both tired but ready for next stage to Cheddar.

Not good news re. Archie though, back in hospital with a chest infection. I wonder when they'll call us for help?

Day 32 27/4 Bawdrip to Blackford

Splott Farm campsite near Blackford	11.5 miles
Sunny, cloud, shower, sun	328 ft

After Emma dropped us off back on the trail, a series of minor roads were followed. As with the day before, cows were a problem and we had to do a long detour at one point. Once it started to rain, we opted to go to the nearest campsite but this meant a lengthy road walk. Then a local farmer stopped and after a chat suggested we use his farm track to get to the site – another kind person just when we needed help. Even better, as we passed the farm he came out and offered a cup of tea so we met his family. Didn't get your name but if you read this, many thanks!

Emma drove us back to Bawdrip on a blue sky warm morning and we set off on a cycle path all nice and leafy.

Good to get going again, first to the village of Crossington, then onto the levels, following narrow roads, very quiet, with right angle bends as in the Fens.

A lovely old way which unfortunately we had to backtrack

At Gold Corner, we set off up a drove road (track) only to find a huge field with cows at the other side of a fence, where we were heading.

Not wanting to risk 'death by cow', we did a 2 mile backtrack / detour and got to a bridge over a 'drain' in time for 2pm Archers, sandwich and a paint (not pint!).

More cows to avoid

The cows were very young and probably harmless. After the break, we had an interminably never ending slog along a road. By 4pm we reached a cross roads and a decision. Too far to go to Cheddar, so decided on trying closer Splott Farm campsite instead. We'd noticed a farm track would ideally be a shortcut, but no right of way. Miraculously a muddy old Land Rover passed, I waved and he stopped and said to use his track. Very friendly bloke and very interested in the challenge*. When we passed his farm he came out and "would we like a cup of tea?". I'd just been saying that to Bob! Had a friendly ½ hour with him and his wife, she's a keen cyclist who we'd waved at earlier. and he knew Gilsland and Carlisle from farm sales. Such a lovely end to the day, to be again 'met' by generous, kind, friendly people very interested in our trek and Barney. Their children sponsored Guide Dogs too.

A short, busy road walk to Splott Farm, where a surprised woman said we could pitch, though she normally did only 'seasonal' caravans and asked us what we normally paid! We gave her £10 and enjoyed pitching, cooking usual, Archers, map reading, planning – a cool night but fine.

---

* He reckoned on seeing 5 or 6 long distance walkers every year.

Day 33 28/4 Blackford to Cheddar

Staying with Karolie who we met on day 4	8.3 miles
Cool start, tiny bit of sleet then sun all day	408 ft

Re-entering 3 days of posts as the app. I'm using gave up last night.
Another sunny day to reach Cheddar where we were put up by Karolie who we met on the SW Coast Path ages ago. With her 3 golden retrievers it was a house full!

Cold bright start with a quick sleet shower as we packed up. We had a dodgy walk on the B3139 road to Blackford, then went for the bridle-path and enjoyed a good track and cow free. Soon coats and over-trousers off as we walked the tree lined track up to Washbrook, then had one scary moment when a 'sleepy' herd in the distance woke up, got up and came in our direction fast! Bob got to the gate and struggled with the binder twine. "Cut it" I said, we made it!* At the next field we dodged another lot, then it was good going on a ridge with gates but no cows, only friendly ponies.

Lunch time visitor

* We retied it.

From our lunch spot on the Brinscombe Hill ridge we looked across to Cheddar Gorge and a large reservoir. Below, a flat area with dairy herds and pasture. Footpath well signed through a farm, so glad to find a deep dyke separated us from a large herd.

In Cheddar we phoned Karolie who we'd met with her dogs on the Cornish cliffs. She welcomed us into her dog run home including 3 gorgeous soft golden retrievers. Barney loved their beds and behaved well, until an argument over a ball, now he is flat out in the bedroom. Another friendly encounter, meal, wine and bed.

Day 34. 29/4 Cheddar to Congresbury

Oak farm campsite, Congresbury	13.9 miles
Rain for ½ hour, then warmed up, blue sky and clear	1789 ft

Up to the top of the Mendips via the path above Cheddar Gorge and some lovely woodland. Then West (the wrong way?) along a ridge, great walking.

15 mile walk today. Lovely day with rain to start as we left Karolie and her dogs. Shopped at Tesco along with 100 school children, an early start. Made our way up Cheddar Gorge road and then by footpath up alongside the gorge, and along the top.

Cheddar Gorge

Delightful woodland, nature reserve walks full of bluebells and birdsong. Not long out of the woods we got onto the Mendips, – rolling hills, rough grassland, tumuli and to the highest point, Beacon Batch, a very 'airy' wide open space. Views to Wales and the Severn bridges – our next goal.

From Beacon Batch, the summit of the Mendips

Did 2 paintings – good sandy heathland tracks up another ridge with a 500BC hill fort. Sun and blue sky day, larks trilling above us. We followed tracks down to cross the very busy A38, then a good bridleway to reach Sandford where a cycle path started…Interesting route round a new Thatchers cider factory – mm... I was thirsty. The cycle path - 'Strawberry Line' was OK, a not too long 3 ½ mile plod, Barney slowing, so Bob carried his food. Lots of reed warblers in sedge – or sedge warblers in reeds!

Must drink lots on hot days

Eventually reached campsite, and the man said they didn't take dogs but I explained that Barney is an assistance dog helping Guide Dogs, and he let us pitch for the night. So here we are, lots of traffic noise and aeroplanes. Bristol tomorrow?

Day 35. 30/4 Congresbury to Bristol

Overnight with friend in Bristol   17.3 miles

Rain shower as we packed up then sun all day.   1166 ft

> I could write pages about today. In brief, a day of contrasts.
> Cycle path / road walking followed by more levels then small hills to Bristol where we stayed for a night with Poppy, Rosie's daughter[*].

At the station, Yatton, we discovered the Strawberry line cafe and what a treat. Delicious coffee and cake, enjoyed outside, and we bought up goodies for the walk. The cafe lady gave us £4 and admired Mr B. We left the village and took a minor road, a bit of a drag but seemed quickest, then it was onto flat fields alongside rivers and only one field had young bullocks so we scared them off OK. Phew.

The Strawberry Line

* Rosie – our friend from home.

The roar of motorway traffic was constant now. After the fields, we came out on a road, having seen no one to talk to until a garden centre and hooray, a cafe. We sat outside for another treat in the sun, cream tea x 2. Very filling, especially as we had uphill to do into a lovely woodland on Tickenham Hill, taking us to the impressive sized Cadbury iron age fort. Cad = a name, bury = fort. It would've been a large settlement with great views all round. We could see the Severn bridges, the Mendips where we'd come from, and the coast, headlands and islands in the Bristol Channel.

On the next page of the map we took a minor road instead of Andy's route and walked past house after house with huge fences and gates, and security cameras watching! On over fields till The Downs School, a very posh prep school where **NO DOGS Allowed** – yet public footpath went right across their playing fields, so we took the route, avoiding a cricket match. We must have looked a sight. More fields, (just sheep) and into steep sided woodland full of bluebells, where we met 4 people and gave cards out.

What a quiet route in between all the housing and roads, leading us down to Easton-in-Gordano and finally the M5 road bridge crossing the River Avon.

We are going slow!

Getting tired of tarmac by now. Rush hour traffic pounding over. It felt weird and quite an achievement reaching the Bristol conurbation – all that way!

Start of the M5 Avon Bridge and a group of teenagers finding out what we're up to

Quite a long trek to find the quiet, tiny Shirehampton station where we waited to catch a train to Poppy's district. More route finding, the GPS finally took us to her house where we sit now, having let ourselves in (note on door, 'key at neighbours'). Poppy was settling her new baby Yoali upstairs, so we made a cup of tea and cooked our instant macaroni. 9:45pm ready for bed, we'll meet her in the morning.

Today was a long 19 miles, we're due for a shorter day.

Posting Ahead

A technique we have used previously on long walks is to post certain items ahead which can then be picked up en route. On this trek we distributed parcels containing supplies by post and in a few cases directly to people whom we would meet en route. Items can be sent direct to Post Offices marked Post Restante (general delivery) for us to pick up as we passed. Mostly however, we posted to family, friends and places we knew we would be visiting, such as pubs and campsites.

To avoid having parcels left for long periods before we were able to retrieve them, we had our 'house sitter', Lucy, send most of the parcels a week or so in advance.

Two sizes of parcels were used, a large envelope and a cardboard box.

All parcels included art paper, guide book sections and maps. The boxes also included food and various other items such as cream for Barney's paws. Stamped and addressed envelopes were also included in all parcels to allow Jos to send completed sketchbooks back home. Postage rates determined the size and weight of the parcels.

This system worked very well and kept us supplied with items we would otherwise had difficulty obtaining locally. Fortunately all parcels arrived and all returned artwork made it back home.

Organising parcel contents, mostly dehydrated meals

Gas cylinders and lithium batteries cannot be sent by post so we had to work out carefully how we could ensure we had adequate supplies.

Day 36, 1/5 Bristol to Pilning

Celia's dog training field.	8.9 miles
Sunshine, coolish	613 ft

More pleasant walking avoiding the built up areas of Bristol and we were directed to a dog friendly cafe.
Then back to flat lands with difficult paths and cows. When looking for somewhere to camp, Celia came to the rescue! By chance she was arriving at her dog training area just as we passed, and has let us camp in her field. Anybody in the Bristol / Gloucester area looking for dog training / agility classes, visit her website for details at caninerelate-bristol.co.uk

Finally met Poppy & Yoali. We all had a good nights sleep. After breakfast, we packed up and walked to the station to catch the train back to Shirehampton. The days walk began, nice weather again. Soon we were off pavements and into parkland – much better.

Dogs

A woman with a dog came to see if we needed any help when she saw us looking at our map. Judy knew Sarah from Guide Dogs and told us of her blind friend Maureen who would've liked to meet us, but had unfortunately fallen downstairs. She told us about good coffee and dog friendly cafe in King Weston. Later we tanked up on very good coffee and croissants, treating ourselves to lush flapjacks and chocolate sludge bar to keep us going.

Very pleasant walking on a ridge, with no sign of Bristol at all, just dog walkers. We dropped down to houses at Henbury and picked up bits and bobs from the Co-Op.

Another good ridge with easy stiles and gates, and no cows, then down to Easter Compton where we had intended to part company with the guidebook and walk to a C&C club site near Almonsbury. We changed our minds, hoping to find a friendly farmer who'd let us camp.

Looked at Blaise hamlet – amazing thatched cottages like Hobbit homes

Then yet more padlocked field gates and tricky stiles for the dog, but he jumped with ease. We were glad to reach a grassy track. A van came up slowly and I flagged it down to ask about camping, the driver Celia said "use my field after I've exercised this lot." She is a dog trainer and very friendly and interested to learn about us. We sat in her fenced off dog agility area and waited for her to run her dogs, then set up our tent in her flat field, with a water tap – all we need.

She said to ring if we wanted anything, we do meet such nice people. So here we are, 3 course meal* inside us, incessant roar and hum of nearby traffic on M5, blackbirds singing in trees. We're crossing the Severn tomorrow – a new chapter begins. Meanwhile Archie losing his hair but playing again.

* Packet of instant soup, dehydrated meal packet, a piece of cake and packet of instant custard.

Day 37. 2/5 Severn Bridge into Wales

Beeches farm campsite north of Chepstow	15.2 miles
Milky grey, calm, slight drizzle later, heavy 10pm	2046 ft

Big day today as we crossed the Severn and entered Wales. Celia suggested a route to the bridge which worked well for us – thanks again!

On reaching Chepstow, we were greeted by Paul from Chepstow Walkers are Welcome (www.walkingchepstow.co.uk) and we certainly were. A fine, dog friendly cafe was just the job along with shops including a pet shop to get a new red collar for Barney. All too soon and we were back in England but not before Paul had taken our picture – thanks Paul. Then we joined Offa's Dyke and eventually reached our campsite for the night but only after Jos painted at Wyntour's Leap where I used to climb many years ago.

Another long day, 16 miles. Began early, 8:30ish and made for Northwick by minor road and over the A403 to the Severn flats, walking towards the old bridge, the new one behind us. A milky, grey light – did 2 paintings.

The old bridge seen from the Severn Flats

Very peaceful, with just the sound of skylarks and hum of motorway. Then up onto the Severn bridge and a long slog across in drizzle, bag felt heavy, or was it the tarmac?

Long walk on the Severn Bridge

Eventually made it to to Chepstow in Wales. In the town, a man stopped and introduced himself – Paul, from a local walking group. He took us to a dog friendly street cafe. We were very ready for coffee, toastie and cake. I went off to a Co-Op and got lost! Also to a pet shop for a red dog collar where friendly staff came out to see Barney.

Welsh Border

Paul showed us the Tourist Office and was very helpful. He took photos of us on the bridge (the Welsh / English border) and we walked back into England!

I restocked with Compeed (just in case...) and then off to follow Offa's Dyke. All very well signed, with easy kissing gates, over meadows, through lovely woodland and on some road. We stopped at Wintour's leap where the edge dropped away vertically. I 'had' to stop and paint:

Bob climbed here 40 or more years ago

When we thought we were nearly at the campsite on a farm, we discovered it was another long mile down a track, which was hard going. Plod plod. On arrival at the friendly reception, £14 (£2 for dog), we were 'booked in' and shown to a peaceful end of the site. The usual phone calls, then tea. Both tired, rain on tent, good to be in, hopefully a shorter day to Monmouth and a rest day. Maybe meet Rosie and Gary, friends from home, visiting south for a wedding.

Navigation

How did we find our way? A variety of means in combination proved successful. On only a few occasions did we go the wrong way normally due to talking when we should have been concentrating on route finding!

Maps

We took 130 1:40000 A4 sheets of the entire route produced by our TrackLogs 1:50000 mapping software. Printing out at 1:40000 scale meant we could see detail without needing reading glasses. The same route was loaded into our mapping GPS.

Guidebooks

Andy Robinson's trail guide includes detailed route descriptions and associated sketch maps for the route not already covered in National Trail guides which we purchased separately.

We sliced up the guides to only carry the route descriptions and any associated maps, saving a lot of weight.

Day 38. 3/5 Chepstow to Monmouth

Monnow Bridge Caravan Site, Monmouth	12.4 miles
Rain eased by 9am, warm day, dry till 5:30 – Very heavy.	2664 ft

Away from motorways. The last few days have been accompanied by the sound of traffic from time to time so it's nice to be back into countryside proper.
A few errors in route finding due to attempting short cuts made for a longer than necessary day and we arrived in a downpour. A nice walk nonetheless.
Met two American ladies who, unusually didn't comment on Barney's pack. Turns out dog panniers are a common sight in the US.
We're now in the campsite near the centre of Monmouth.

Spring woodland with bluebells in profusion

Later start as we waited for rain to ease. Route arguing – both tired! Finally got underway, met 2 chatty American ladies who'd backpacked north to south on Offa's Dyke. Had very light loads. Our route mostly alongside river Wye, lovely, magical – trees, birdsong and warm, felt like walking abroad.

We continued up a ridge through fantastic bluebell woods, banks of them, and then across fields, all easy gates and stiles.

The Wye valley on the way to Monmouth

We wished we'd taken a river Wye path the last 3 miles, as Offa's Dyke went uphill steeply, then back down steeply. Rain began as we entered Monmouth, we bought fish & chips and ate them in a torrential downpour. Found the tiny town campsite and knocked on the door of a house as office closed. Grumpy woman signed us in and told me to take wet dog out of the office! However she told us to pitch by a shed we can use, with a little shelter and seat. We are very public, surrounded by campers and caravans. A few noisy kids, oh well every night is different.

Day 39. 4/5 Rest day in Monmouth

We've been walking for 10 days since the last break so today we took it easy. Barney was happy.

First thing, Rosie and Gary turned up on their way home from a wedding and they brought some coffee – a great way to start the day. Rosie sent us on our way at the start of the adventure when she took us to the station in March.

After washing clothes etc. we met up with Gerry by chance, a guide dog user and had a very interesting chat. Thanks Gerry for taking the time to see us and tell us something about what guide dogs mean to you.

A few drinks, some food then shopping and the day's gone.

£25 collected. Lovely start – a lie in.

Card 4

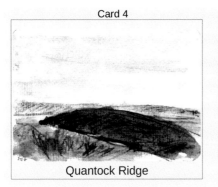

Quantock Ridge

Hi Jane, I think this is no. 4!?
We were at a trig point on highest hill on the Quantock Ridge & I'm looking to a tumuli barrow, Northish with S. Wales & Bristol Channel! Seems ages ago now – look at www.huntstile organic farm to see where we stayed that night – all for free! A very upmarket Burnlaw. This morning we were visited by Rosie & Gary!! They've been nearby for another wedding (yurts, tepees!) so lovely to see them. I miss my friends! Wouldn't it be lovely if you could join us – a tiny tent! & light sl.bag – we got cooker. Cont'd on next card no 5→ →!! love Jos xx

Then Rosie & Gary turned up – such hugs and smiles!

Enjoying real coffee

We had their strong coffee and sat in our 'shed' catching up – so lovely to see my dear friend. Then on with camp life... washing and drying out stuff in very welcome sunshine. Slow start and time went, nice to catch up on jobs.

Later we met a guy who does guide dog puppy training. We were introduced to his 20th pup! How dedicated, a fine looking Labradoodle. Again really interesting to learn about what they do, training a pup from 8 weeks old.

Card 5

Bank Holiday Monday, Monmouth

Cont'd! Card No 5?
BLUEBELL Woods on Offa's Dyke, between Chepstow & Monmouth. Lovely river Wye – high cliffs Bob once climbed – Wintour's Leap gr8 looking down on Wye curves. yest(Sun) balmy walk along river then up on Offas ridge in woods full of bluebells. Got soaked at end of day getting into Monmouth – now on a little site right in town, having a Bank Hol Mon. off. Just seen Rosie & Gary! Now washing to do! Barney asleep in tent, ready to stay put all day! Next some long hilly days – Welsh – Black Mountains, Pandy – Hay on Wye – Knighton – All going well, hoping in Oz too – much love Jos xxxx & Bny

Gerry with her wonderful Guide / hearing dog

We enjoyed a wander through the town and by chance met Gerry, who is sight and hearing impaired. Her guide dog, a German Shepherd / Retriever cross has been trained as a Guide and Hearing dog. She chatted for an hour with us about the difference her dog makes to life. Good to hear that, we learn more every time we meet a sight impaired person.

So here we are, night time, and had 2 pints in town, a Mexican meal, no tea to cook. Rain hammering down. Long walk to Pandy tomorrow.

Day 40. 5/5 Monmouth to Pandy

Rising Sun pub, Pandy	16.5 miles
On and off rain on way, wind and rain evening	1980 ft

What a difference gates make instead of stiles! We made quick progress as we didn't need to keep taking Barneys panniers and harness off.
Battery flat so that's it for now.

Very wet during night, I lay awake listening to the rain. Bob keen to get up at 6:30 (unusually early for him). We were away by 8:30*, and through the streets and outskirts following the Offa's signs.

On the way to Pandy

The walk was good, as well signed with easy gates so no hold up with stiles. Mainly woodland to start then we followed the river Trothy, a stream in spate. Sun out briefly, a cloud followed us and gusty wind so we put our Lite-Speeds[†] on. More up and down through fields with quiet cows, quiet everywhere with just a few very minor roads. Rain began in earnest the last few miles, so on with the Gore-Tex and head down – very green fields and red mud.

Eventually reached Pandy by 5ish and found the pub, the Rising Sun - no dogs allowed in pub until I said he is an assistance dog helping Guide Dogs! We put the tent up in driving rain, glad to get inside and brew tea and warm up.

Now writing this in the pub, full up after butternut squash soup, lovely beef stew and treacle tart and ice cream. Phew. Barney is drying out by a radiator. Might stay another day as forecast rough tomorrow.

* From getting up to leaving always seems to take us about 2 hours
† Very lightweight wind / shower proof jackets.

Day 41. 6/5 Rest day in Pandy. Rain all day.

A bad forecast for the next stage which goes up to 2300ft in height, so we decided to stay put for the day.
A morning of rain allowed us to fester in the tent – a happy Barney!
Then Frank, Community Fundraiser for Guide Dogs Cymru, joined us in the tent - a brave man. We learnt yet more about Guide dogs, all of it quite remarkable. He then took some pics of us with his 'demo' dog. Not sure if you can see it but at one point I think Barney thought it was something to eat!

Lazy start, rain. Good festering day – reading Kindle (at last) and a visit to tent by Welsh guy from Cardiff Guide Dogs. Fascinating to hear more about guide dog training – such a worthwhile cause.

Artificial Guide Dog

I rang Dan in Australia (at work) and good to hear him. He's glad to be back home, but more Melbourne hospital next Monday.

Another friendly night in the pub, smiley landlady – Barney charmed his way in! More donations from local couple.

106

Day 42 7/5 Pandy to Hay-on-Wye

Campsite near Boatside Farm, Hay-on-Wye	18.1 miles
Bright start, showers on hill, sun	2621 ft

Apparently it's election day. We 'elected' to walk to Hay on Wye and what a superb walk it was. 10 miles of ridge walking in countryside like home in the North Pennines. It's the highest we've been so far, at 2300ft.

We were joined by John who is walking Offa's Dyke and we were all able to stroll along a well made up path.

Arrived in Hay at 6 and were just walking out when I spotted staff in a cafe laughing at Barney with his panniers (he gets smiles wherever he goes). We make a point of giving one of our cards to anybody who reacts to Barney, they responded with a donation, 2 cups of tea and two slices of cake! All this and they were shut – many thanks to the staff of Eve Victoria cafe in Hay on Wye and may you have a successful time through the upcoming festival.

Election Day!

Another trig. point

Fine start, off by 8am for our long hill walk, along the Hatterrall Ridge, starting up steep lanes, till out on the ridge, land dropping to valleys either side. Met another walker at the first trig point, John who accompanied us part way. He had heard about us!

Good walking on the ridge

Rain showers came and went and it was cool with wind, but great views of hills (Black Mountains) – reminding us of the Pennines.

Sugar Loaf seen from the Hatterrall Ridge

It felt like home with an airy sense of space and the long moorland track, pity it was made up gravel in parts though. At the last hill, we dropped steeply down to a lane, back into warmer climes, fields, lanes and down suddenly into Hay on Wye looking so interesting with all the bookshops. We found a Spar. A cafe was closing up and smiley girls looking at Barney – we went over to them and they asked if we'd like a cuppa tea and carrot cake. Lovely, friendly, young lasses – Eva Victoria it was called. More Guardian Angels, they gave us £5 too.

We crossed the Wye – looking wide now, and uphill to a nice campsite – John already there and a German girl who's done LeJog and 3 U.S. Long Distance Trails. Goodness knows what else!

We had a treat – Thatchers cider with our meal.

Day 43 8/5 Hay on Wye to Kington

Overnight in Worcester with family	15.6 miles
Became steadily wetter	2353 ft

Today was marked by two churches at Newchurch and Gladestry, both welcomed walkers with tea and coffee! Very welcome as it started to rain at the first and was steady by the second. Hergest Ridge followed and then we were greeted by brother Mick who was waiting to drive us to Worcester. A night in Worcester for a family gathering – it was great to see everybody.

Now at Worcester, at Mick's house, having a lively get together of Mahons & Tookes, a good laugh too!

Up at 6am and away by 8am. Walk by a big curving Wye, then mixed woodland, lane and field. Rain held off but quite close. We stopped to make coffee at a church, a great idea, welcoming walkers.

A welcome break for walkers in the church

Met other Offa's Dyke walkers, one woman was very taken by Barney and took a card. More easy walking with variety, all good gates and signs but then the rain started, so lunch and cuppa tea sheltering in another church. I painted a stained glass window. Great to be out of the rain, then a steep uphill, but good gradient up on to the Hergest Ridge and fast striding along.

Clouds, so not much view, at the end of the road was Mick!

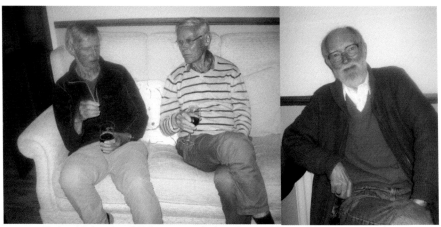
Bob with brother Mick contemplating the world's problems over a pint.
My brother Steve, just contemplating!

Card 6  Friday 8th	Dear Jane, Having sarnies in a church on way to Kington – a wet day today – yesterday lovely hill walk from Pandy in Wales to Hay on Wye – felt like Pennines up on tops – long stride 10 miles – 19 altogether! Black Mountains – all unfamiliar, job to get bearings – where is Cross Fell!! Night with bro's at Worcester. Bobs bro. picked us up – my bro. over too so lively get together. Back on walk Sat-to Knighton then Shrops! Lots of Love Jos xx

Day 44 9/5 Kington to Knighton

Field / farm campsite next to railway line, Knighton	15.4 miles
Clear, mostly sunny day, but wind on the tops. Warm in valleys. DRY.	2804 ft

A special day – we weren't carrying our sacks.
Nephew Steve and family picked us up and took us back to Kington, then walked with us for part of the way – that is after we got lost in Kington first!
Mick was waiting for us at Knighton with our bags in the car – Barney wasn't very impressed as he thought he'd seen the last of his panniers. He promptly jumped into the back of the car expecting to be taken home!

A family night at Worcester with the bros. including mine and Sheila, also Penny, Ian and boys along with Chris & Jude[*]. We were picked up in the morning by Steve, Geraldine, Sean & Shane. They drove us back to Kington, where we dithered around getting lost with too much chatting! Finally underway, uphill out of Kington, we had a picnic together before they turned back.

Steve, Geraldine, Sean and Shane with us for the day

* Niece and nephews along with their families.

Offa's Dyke became a mound to walk on. At last the weather gave us great views of hills near and far. Woodland and small green fields, sheep and lambs in many of them, very pastoral and no bloody cows! Good gate 'stiles' most of the way.

From one high point we could look back to our wet days route and see the tall clump of monkey puzzle trees on the Hergest Ridge we'd tramped along in the rain, - Friday, the day Cameron got back in Grrrr..

Wales or England – switching back and forth

Today we were in Borderland, into Powys, all so very lush and quiet following the Dyke. Eventually down hill to Knighton where we met Mick with our big sacks, they do seem heavy after just carrying day sacks. Barney bounced along with no sacks. Must keep an eye on the cyst / growth I've found on his jaw – oh dear, hope it's not a problem.

The farm campsite is very quiet so far, we're pitched next to a railway line!

Section 3. The Midlands and the Peak

Knighton to Edale

3 nights with friends, 1 'wild' camp and 9 in campsites	150.9 miles
Mixed spring weather, some days warm, some days wet.	17215 ft

A varied, rural route, leaving hill country to cross agricultural lowland, mainly by footpath, canal tow path, amazingly avoiding built up areas. We reached The Peak District and beloved hills once more.

We left Offa's Dyke Trail and walked in a NE direction through Shropshire and Staffordshire, the route taking us along the flower rich, wooded Wenlock Edge to the once industrial area around Ironbridge. We crossed the river

Severn once more, at Coalport. Then across farmland, around fields of crops, wheat, barley, passing acres of poly tunnels full of strawberries.

Midlands farming country

The thick hedgerows full of birdsong, warblers, tits, wren, thrush and blackbirds, giving us beautiful dawn choruses to wake us early! We met and followed The Staffordshire Way, by The Staffordshire & Worcestershire Canal at Penkridge, enjoying peaceful canal towpath walking, accompanied by slow chugging barges and people relaxing on holiday.

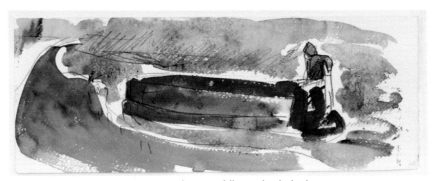

Barge 'sped' past while we had picnic

We crossed the wooded heathland of Cannock Chase, and walked alongside The Trent Mersey Canal as we made our way to Uttoxeter, where we camped in the middle of the racecourse! At last we began to head Northwards, following the river Dove, leading us back to the hills through the beautiful limestone area of Dovedale. Arriving at Edale in The Peak District, we reached the southern end of the Pennine Way. From here, ever Northwards, along the spine of England, over peat bog studded upland, vast stretches of windswept moorland. We passed conurbations including Sheffield, Manchester and Huddersfield, hardly knowing they were there, except for crossing Trans-Pennine motorways reminding us of another world!

From Mam Tor, to Hollins Cross

We found it uplifting reaching Derbyshire, once more the sound of home, the call of a curlew, and sight of stone walls again.

Day 45 10/5 Knighton to Craven Arms

With friends at Church Stretton	15.3 miles
Warm and dry!	2901 ft

Met another End to Ender today! Stuart is doing the same route and was in the Knighton campsite last night.

A hilly walk again as we headed away from the Welsh Border and into Shropshire. On the way down one hill we came across some 4 wheel drive enthusiasts struggling to get up the track – it would have been much easier walking.

The guide book suggested that the tearoom at Abcott was the best on the whole trail so we had to stop! Stuart, the other LEJOGer turned up so we talked shop over excellent tea and cake.

Onto Craven Arms where old friends Hilary and Mike picked us up to stay with them – luxury!

The farm campsite we left today was very basic but all we needed, a field, a clean loo and water. A train whooshed by in the evening very close. This morning, a friendly woman collected our money, and talked about living up north and playing music. She said her name is June Tabor! (a well known folk singer)

The path does exist

We had another 'green' walk up hill and down dale – quite long ups! Tiny hamlets, old churches, fields full of sheep and lambs, woodland, forest. Behind us, views of hills south we'd walked. Before us, north, lay the Shropshire hills.

Rocke Cottage Tearooms

We stopped at the recommended tea house and enjoyed strong Shropshire tea and cake where we met Stuart who is also doing Lejog, with an ultralight pack. Mine is 13.2Kg without water!

Now at Hilary & Mike's[*] in their large, very beautifully decorated and very tidy home. Bed time after a lovely meal and chat.

Day 46 11/5 Craven Arms to Rushbury

With friends at Church Stretton	9.7 miles
Sunny and warm	1321 ft

An easy day as Mike dropped us off and picked us up at the start and end of the walk – good man! Hilary also accompanied us and we had only day sacks so it was very pleasant apart from one near miss with cows.

Mike kindly took us to Craven Arms and Bob, Hilary & I, as in the 'old days' walked together, by river meadows, avoiding cows and up a track onto

* Hilary & Mike are old friends. Jos & Hilary studied Fine Art at the University of Newcastle Upon Tyne

the Wenlock Edge. It was a woodland walk with flowers: bluebells, garlic, anemones, violets, all beneath the dappled shade of the trees.

I painted from our lunch log – needed time to take in the patterns of light and dark. I don't often paint woodland.

On Wenlock Edge

There was time to shop in Church Stretton, before tea together in their lovely garden. Really nice to renew contact with such dear old friends.

Day 47, 12/5 Rushbury to Ironbridge

Ironbridge Power Station campsite!	13.7 miles
Warm, sunny and breezy	1501 ft

First, thanks to our hosts of the last couple of nights, Hilary and Mike. We're eating Hilary's home made cake right now.

Then, great to meet Jo and all the other people on the trail today, thanks for all the donations, both from today and all previous days, now more than £100.

Next, Much Wenlock where we were welcomed in the Copper Kettle Cafe and Wenlock Hardware who both donated as well as cream tea and glue! I'll let you work out which one was from which! Also, the cafe is now collecting for Barney. Much Wenlock is definitely a place we will be coming back to...

Finally, we're camped next to a power station – can't be bad!

Hilary dropped us off where we 'left off' yesterday. The walk seemed long – through trees on a bridleway, once a railway line, thankfully not a tarmac cycle route, so not bad underfoot.

Time to leave Hilary & Mike

We had a brief view of a hill called The Wrekin but no time for sketching as already stopped for lunch break.

Copper Kettle Tea Rooms

Much relieved to get to Much Wenlock, where we met very friendly people.

Had cream tea in the Copper Kettle, and when the waitresses learnt about Barney, they said to put cost of tea (£9) to our funds. They also took a photo for the cafe Facebook page.

Next, the hardware shop wouldn't take payment for a mat I bought for £6!

We plodded on in sunshine out of Much Wenlock, through fields and woods until finally this bizarre site for the tent:

Day 48,13/5 Ironbridge to Tong

Tong Hill Farm front garden!

Sunny and warm all day

15.3 miles

1556 ft

A notable day, first getting to Ironbridge itself and then coffee at Darby's next to the bridge where Thea found us. Thea has been following the blog and when she saw we were in Ironbridge decided to try and find us – well spotted!
Next the interesting industrial heritage before we struck out across footpaths.
The heat slowed us all down so by the time we got to Tong Norton we'd had enough. Jos made some enquiries at the pub and we had an invite from a local farmer at the bar to camp in his garden; thanks Tom.

Left the 'power station' camp / caravan site, heading uphill to rejoin the route through woodland, until we dropped down to Ironbridge, where we crossed the famous bridge.

Halfway across I spotted a coffee shop with outside tables. No sooner had we started drinking and I sketching, a woman excitedly introduced herself and said 'There you are Barney!'

She'd been following us on the blog, knew we'd be in Ironbridge and came out to look for us! Thea is a mad keen flatcoat owner and we talked about flatcoats for quite a while! The Darby's cafe gave us a donation too and we took photos – so a slow start…

We got a bit 'off track' leaving Ironbridge, negotiating our way around groundworks, houses and fields.

Darby's 1774 Tearoom

Green fields after Ironbridge

After a lunch stop, Barney slowed with the heat, so Bob took his bags and harness and he moved much better. Still a long way to go, we decided to make for the pub at Tong Norton. I went inside and asked the locals if they knew the farmer at Tong Hill farm and he, (Tom) was at the bar! Said yes, we could camp on his lawn and he gave us directions. Phew.

We walked through his horse fields and found the farm, where a friendly couple made us tea in the kitchen and we had a chat with Tom who'd given up his dairy herd 20 years ago. Here we are, pitched on the lawn, M54 motorway traffic in the distance and birds settling down in trees. Another long day! Time for sleep.

Day 49, 14/5 Tong to the A5

Whitegate Farm campsite past Bishops Wood	5.1 miles
Rain most of day	305 ft

The forecast was for heavy rain so we opted for a short day and just walked to what was originally yesterday's destination. We only had limited food as a result but surprise, surprise the site also had a farm shop, so we indulged! Barney has slept all day through what turned out to be light rain, Jos read and caught up with the Archers and I published Barney's Story!

As for the walk, two things of note – we are now in Staffordshire and we have crossed the watershed.

Short morning walk, bridle paths and road – so good to set up camp at 11am!

Leaving Shropshire

All ready for a relax in the tent. Whitegate Farm has a wonderful farm shop with so much tempting food, fruit, veg, pies, cakes, biscuits and a very friendly chappie. We began with pork pie and Parkin! Mmm... strawberry and cream for pud, and a scotch egg thing and corn on the cob!

Lorraine from Dogs Unite rang as we were arriving and we plan to meet up tomorrow in Cannock Chase. I'm sleepy after reading H is for Hawk on my Kindle.

Barney's Story

We've met many people who are now following Barney's trip so I thought I'd tell his story for those of you who don't know it.

Barney came from Flatcoat Re-homing[*] in 2008. Our last flatcoat had died of old age 6 months before and we were missing the presence of a dog in the home and on our walks. Jos, one November day was walking alone on a vast windswept Northumbrian beach and came across a man with one or two flatcoats enjoying themselves in the waves. Like all flatcoat owners (when they spot another flatcoat), she couldn't resist saying hello! He told Jos that if she wanted to see more, then to call in at the pub at the end of the beach (The Ship Inn, Newton) where the landlady has two and is mad keen on the breed.

Jos takes over:

Christine at the pub, brought her beautiful Silas downstairs to show me and we had a good chat. One thing I'll always remember is her saying "The thing about flatcoats is they make you smile, every morning when you get up!".

That night, when back, I googled Flat Coat Rescue and found the phone number for the co-ordinator, Brian Jones in Leicestershire. He asked questions about our suitability. Having had one before, we knew their characteristics, boundless energy, enthusiasm for life, their friendliness with people and dogs... I could go on. They don't like being left alone for long, especially if just one dog, both of us worked from home, so no problem there... and yes, have a large garden, live in the Northumbrian countryside and love walking. We must have ticked all the right boxes and YES, he had a young dog, not quite 2 years old, looking for a new home.

We learnt that he'd come from a very loving home, but due to unforeseen circumstances, they sadly had to part with him. He had already been out to two potential new owners but was soon returned by both as he was found to be just too much, too big and too boisterous (unsettled of course), fortunately for us! We travelled south to meet him at Brian's kennels and it was 'love at first sight' when he cantered down the corridor towards me, leapt up, putting his front paws on my shoulders, giving me a big lick! A couple of days later, he was jumping in the back of the car for the journey to his new home up North.

He certainly took some settling in too, training him not to eat or chase our old cats and hens! Also, not to pull my arm out of its socket on a lead walk! I enrolled on Obedience Level 1 Gun Dog classes locally, and we worked hard, bonding all the time.

* Flatcoated Retriever Society Rescue, Rehousing and Welfare Scheme.

At home he is out daily walking the North Pennine moors with me. He doesn't like the heat or road walking, but does like eating tissues people have dropped, and vegetables out of the garden, especially lettuce and carrots!

Soon, we introduced him to the tent and backpacking with us. His first big trip was almost his last when he showed us his love of rolling on his back in snow, unfortunately on the cornice on top of a mountain! He has clocked up over 220 Munros (Scottish mountains 3000ft and over) with over 70 of them on backpacking trips so he became very used to the tent and the routine of wild camping. Barney accompanied us on the last section of the Cape Wrath Trail from Torridon to Cape Wrath and also backpacked over all the Scottish 4000ft mountains in one trip from Cairngorm to Ben Nevis – he likes mountains!

I am an artist who loves working outdoors and Barney always accompanies me over Pennine Moors and to Scottish Islands on art trips! He would settle, be quietly on watch by my side as soon as I got the art stuff out to paint. Always my constant companion.

As Brian later wrote 'It was a match made in heaven!'.

Day 50, 15/5 A5 to Cannock Chase

Springslade C&C Club site, Cannock Chase	14.2 miles
Warm, shorts and T shirts all day!	768 ft

Lorraine from Guide Dogs, Dogs Unite arranged to travel up from Reading to spend some time with us today. We eventually met up outside Penkridge Co-op and had a very pleasant walk to Bednall.
More interest and donations at the Star Inn, Penkridge and at Bednall.
A change of scenery for us with a canal walk, another slow pace of life, like walking!

Up at 6am and set off by 8am away from NOISY A5. Chatted to lady at the farmhouse and with help of her young daughters, took photos of us for their Facebook page!

We had a rural walk on the well marked Staffordshire Way next to arable crops. I stopped to paint a line of poplars and a tree for Jane! Some lovely nature reserve trees, wetland, more fields and a road walk taking us into Penkridge and the Co-Op shop! Warm again.

Lorraine from Dogs Unite joined us

Good to meet up with Lorraine Joseph from Dogs Unite. She accompanied us on our walk by a canal, lovely to see longboats and locks working.

This one's for Cath!

Any food in there?

A brief stop so I could paint, then on over more farmland, no cows – just crops! Very rural and peaceful, yet motorway not far away.

Under the M6 Motorway

On reaching the village of Bednall, Lorraine left us to return home.

We had a long walk on a busy road in Cannock Chase, it was a relief to get to Springslade campsite in the forest. Quiet at first but filling up fast as it's Friday night.

We've all got tired feet / paws! Barney very slow on last 2 miles, mustn't push him too much, hopefully shorter day tomorrow.

| Card 7

15/5 Day 50 | Dear Jane – This tree stood out in middle of a field, as we made our way from the A5 to Penkridge – it didn't fit on the card!! Our route cleverly takes us on tracks & ways through woods & alongside field edges, so we are unaware of the big towns & motorways near. We enjoyed walking by canals – the Shropshire & Trent / Mersey with peaceful barges chugging along. Today a girl 'driving' one, stopped & let her flatcoat 'River' come out & meet Barney!! He was 2 & very lively. She said she'd seen us on Facebook!!!! More agricultural land to Uttoxeter then Peak District – Dovedale. That will be lovely. Good to get txts from my friends faraway! xxx |

Day 51. 16/5 Cannock Chase to Abbots Bromley

Little Dunstal farm hideaway site past Abbots Bromley, no facilities	13 miles
Warm day, shorts but cool breeze	695 ft

A day of sports – bikes, horses, joggers, sailing, even shooting!
After Cannock Chase, the Trent Mersey canal took us towards Rugeley before we headed north again. More barges including one belonging to Helen who had a flatcoat on board! She even knew about us from the flatcoat Facebook page!
Then it was onto Abbots Bromley via Blithfield reservoir and hence the sailing sports!

Slept well, quiet site after all, up at 6am but not off till 9 as gave ourselves headaches studying the route ahead to coincide with friends Robin & Gwyn.

Social Media

Once we had decided to raise money for Guide Dogs, Social Media became an important part of the trek. Previous treks by others with an online presence have shown the power of social media in attracting and sustaining an interested audience. It didn't take long to decide on a name, given the charity we were supporting, and BarneysLongWalk was born! First as a blog and then following on soon after, a dedicated Facebook page. It was necessary to do both as we had friends and relatives who didn't use Facebook but we knew that potentially it could attract more interest. Both can be found by searching for BarneysLongWalk. Both have dedicated apps. which I installed and configured for use on Bob's smartphone.

Once set up, preparation for the trip was routinely posted to both systems. Everything was fine before we started, things changed somewhat as we progressed. Bob found posting to the blog using the Blogger app. was fine for text but could be very frustrating when posting an entry which included pictures. Loss of mobile phone connection would mean all the previously entered text was lost resulting in a retype, sometimes several times. Facebook on the other hand suffered no such losses and was more straightforward to use. In theory, the text could be copy and pasted but this also proved problematic.

Both of our phones were using the Vodafone network as we have found that it offered the most complete coverage in the Scottish Highlands. In retrospect, it would have been better to split the phones between different service providers as Vodafone coverage was often only 'basic' and limited when uploading images, hence the problems just mentioned.

Regular inclusion of references to our JustGiving donation page resulted in finally raising over £7000 for Guide Dogs – worth the effort.

'BarneysLongWalk' blog and Facebook page created an online group of followers which grew steadily as we headed north. Guide Dogs, via its Dogs Unite website updated its users of our progress and overall we developed quite a following. Barney's Facebook page for example still has over 800 followers!

At times, updating both the blog and Facebook page was challenging – mobile coverage was not always reliable!

PS Jos kept to notebooks and Biro for her daily diary, not forgetting her sketchbook record all the way.

The first bit of today's walk was very pleasant, through woodland, silver birch then pine and a stream running alongside, people jogging, mountain biking, horse riding, bird watching. We left Cannock Chase and walked alongside the Trent and Mersey Canal and River Trent alongside too. Barges chugging along, all very peaceful. They go slower than us!

Flatcoats

One girl from a houseboat said "Oh I must let my flatcoat out" and out came a 2 year old gangly, River! She (Helen) lived on her barge and had seen us on the Flatcoat Facebook page.

We enjoyed the canal towpath, the walk became more tiring in heat on roads, so stopped for a pint… of orange at a village pub, then more roads and fields over to Blithfield Reservoir.

Blithfield Reservoir.

Next, Abbots Bromley, and a long uphill lane to the field we are now in with one tap! Sound of traffic in distance. A milking herd were close nearby (behind electric fence!) but they all walked off for milking. Barney tired too, I'm a bit out of sorts, well tired, legs ache. Good to be in tent by 5pm.

Day 52.17/5. Abbots Bromley to Uttoxeter

Uttoxeter Race Course!	6.7 miles
Warm, sun then cloud, cool!	304 ft

We were camped a mile outside the village so still no pub in the evening!
We went to the farm to pay and the kind lady gave a donation – many thanks.
Also the knowledge that we could take a short cut to our route without going all the way back to the village.
A short day of 7 miles as we needed a break. Luckily it wasn't race day as we would not have been able to get onto the campsite!
A trip into town for provisions and a much welcome couple of pints and a meal in the Dapple Grey where we were treated like royalty and had our photo taken! Many thanks for the donations from both pub and customers – people are so kind. The walk was mostly over fields so only one pic!

Good sleep and we had lie in till 6:30! Sunny so put shorts on. We left at 8:30 and walked up the road to Little Dunstall Farm to pay our £2.50 fee and also see if we could walk on the private track. Met a very friendly Mrs farmer and 3 springers, we talked dogs and when she heard what we were doing, handed our money back! Later she caught us up on the track and 'parped' and gave us a £10 note! We are coming across such spontaneous generosity.

Big fields to walk beside

The track took us directly to the Staffordshire Way, then it was alongside crops, over stiles into pasture and past a few herds of sleepy dairy cows. It wasn't long before we reached the outskirts of Uttoxeter. We thought how green everything is, barley, grass, trees, woods in all shades, all so rural, yet but a 'step' away from nearby towns.

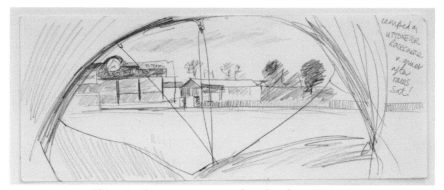

Uttoxeter Racecourse campsite, view from the tent

A friendly reception at the racecourse which was very quiet after a busy race day on Saturday. We put the tent up on the campsite in the centre of the racecourse!

Then off to Tesco and a Marstons pub, the Dapple Grey, again barely a second after mentioning what we are doing, the manager said put cost of your meal and beer towards the charity, we'll take a photo and put you on our Facebook page!

After 2 pints and a good meal, now back at tent. Another experienced walker, Lyndon, camped nearby and is walking Weymouth to Cape Wrath and back via the Hebrides, collecting for Birmingham Children's Hospital. He's done LEJOG – so that's a sign, once you start, you can't stop!

Day 53. 18/5. Uttoxeter to Thorpe

Ashbourne Heights campsite past Thorpe	17.9 miles
Wet most of day	1994 ft

A long day of 19 miles with the first 5 hours steady rain but it improved after we got past JCB country (Rocester). First woodland and then onto higher ground and we heard a curlew!
Reaching Thorpe we crossed the bridge over the Dove to enter Derbyshire.

It rained in the night and a wet start. We packed up, and away by 8:15 all togged up. Soon out of Uttoxeter and on through fields next to river Dove – stiles too big! Bob had to lift the dog over 2 or 3 times and got quite fed up. We did a wrong turn and walked through a posh Prep school (again!). Rain eased by midday and a nice walk by the river, then into lovely woodland, bluebells, garlic, until we crossed farmland to rejoin the Limestone Way. Heard first curlew since home. After a week of walking (from Ironbridge), through the rural part of the Midlands by canals, in woods, fields, we now see hills and limestone outcrops ahead.

We crossed the River Dove today and entered Derbyshire. A steep hill walk up to village of Thorpe, where we met a walking group with a guide, CF or HF holidays. One man gave us £20, another couple with a labrador £3 and then another couple with a golden retriever / poodle cross (a Goodle??) £10 – all within one hour!

Cows near the road

Reached campsite at Ashbourne Heights after 19 miles. Very glad to arrive and get tent up by 7 for usual meal, except cider and beer from a very well stocked shop. Barney did well today, probably because it's cooler.

Day 54. 19/5. Ashbourne Heights to Biggin

Waterloo Inn pub garden, Biggin	10.2 miles
Rain, showers, sun	2035 ft

First, we met up with staff at the Ashbourne Heights site where we camped overnight and had a welcome coffee. Thanks for the donation – may see you in Scotland.
The walk was a day of sunshine and showers through Dovedale and onwards to Milldale where we had more coffee, the day's turning out pretty good.
We eventually stopped early at the Waterloo Inn, Biggin, camping behind a pub was too good to miss!

Staff very friendly and gave us £15 fee back for Guide dogs! Made us coffee and wished us luck – such warm hearted people we meet. All posed for photos:

We were soon into Dovedale and very beautiful with a dramatic cone shaped hill 'Thorpe Cloud' with a steep sided gorge, stepping stones across the River Dove.

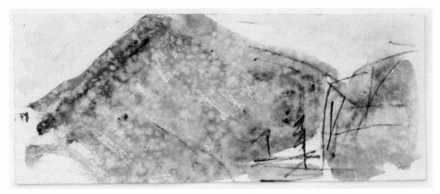

Stopped to paint and down came rain, so a very minimal result

Enjoyed walk alongside the river on a good path, the water falling in steps all the time, saw dippers, ducks, and warblers on the river.

At Milldale, a hamlet by the river, we stopped at Polly's Kitchen and bought TREATS – coffee, hot pasty and cake – Bakewell Tart. Sat on a bench to enjoy, then on we go with occasional rain, bit heavy, but well sheltered by trees. We turned up a 'dry valley', Biggindale, and sat for lunch in sunshine watching squirrels. Redstarts were there according to a couple we met, but we didn't see them.

Not that old!

Dove Dale stepping stones

At Biggin we decided to camp at the Waterloo Inn and managed to ring and book in – hooray, they do take dogs after all. I was saying we have an assistance dog! So here we are, tent up, washing drying and waiting for pub to open at 6pm, Nice one! Mmm... tomato with basil soup, veg, lasagne, salad, new potatoes, cheesecake and 3 samples of different beers.

Day 55. 20/5 Biggin to Blackwell

Beech Croft Farm campsite, Blackwell	17.7 miles
Showers on and off, cleared up, lovely sunny evening	2068 ft

A long day of over 18 miles so we were happy to get to the camp site.
We've seen more walkers today than we have see for the last month, it's definitely walking country!
A special thanks to the Rotherham Metro Ramblers for the impromptu collection as we passed on the Limestone Way. I meant to get a photo of you all for the blog, perhaps you could arrange for another walk so we meet again...
The countryside feels much more like home now – we're heading towards home!
We had some new comments on Barney's pack today including 'is he carrying his pyjamas'!

After a road start, we were on tracks and fields and all stiles easy, with stone gaps or small gates. Enjoyed a lovely quiet dry valley, Gratton Dale, and met a walking group all very interested in Barney – "Does he have his pyjamas in his bags?" That's a new one!

On way to Youlgrave we had lunch on a bridge over pools of dammed river, beautiful green reflections, I could have painted and watched birds, but we had a long walk ahead so no 'dallying' about.

Out of Youlgrave, another walking group, the Rotherham Metro Ramblers stopped and fired off questions and all dug into pockets and gave us £30 or so! Lots of warm wishes, then the Limestone Way, now a delight to get a good pace going striding along on green 'sward' and sacks don't feel so heavy. Open spaces and hill top views again with easy gate stiles so no hold ups. Dropped steeply down steps to one dry valley and back up to an old farmyard where ice cream sold in a barn, £2 in honesty box.

Next treat, a mug of tea and scones outside Moneyash cafe. After that, hard work covering ten miles on roadsides up hill, a long way – ouch!

Tent Problem

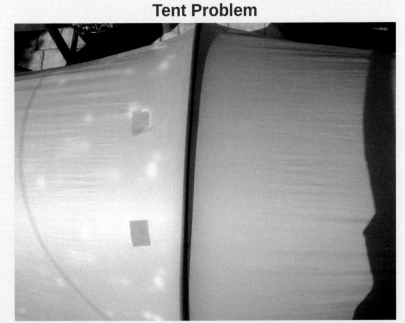

As we progressed on the walk, it became apparent that our tent had a problem. Over the last few years, we had seen mysterious lighter coloured circles appearing on one flysheet section. Initially disregarded, we realised that they could be a serious problem – the material was slowly disintegrating where they existed. We used temporary repair patches where the material had degenerated to the point that the flysheet would leak. Fortunately it's inherent strength meant it wouldn't completely fail.

Whilst staying with Robin, he was able to take some detailed photographs of the problem which we emailed to the tent supplier, but to no avail. The problem got worse as we progressed and by the time we reached John o' Groats the flysheet was a patchwork of repairs!

I later emailed Hilleberg directly but they could offer no satisfactory reason why the circles appeared – note they were only on one section of the flysheet, the other sections showed no sign of the problem. We have regularly treated the flysheet with the recommended protection to reduce ultraviolet damage which occurs with tents exposed to sunlight.

My thoughts are that the particular section came from a different manufacturing batch which resulted in the problem. That said, the tent did serve us well for 6 years of regular backpacking trips and survived (just) the 1400 miles / 4 months of this trip!

Monyash

Once on the tops, looking back South were long horizons of hills we've walked. To the north, bigger hills, the start of the Pennines.

The countryside is starting to look familiar to us

We romped along to find the campsite at Blackwell. Very friendly, very clean and lovely situation, then tea, soup, couscous, custard and cake!

Day 56. 21/5 Day off. Bob's birthday.

A day off. We were picked up by our friend Robin and taken around various outdoor shops to get Jos some new boots after her old Meindls started to leak. Various repairs etc and then a lovely meal with Robin and his wife Gwynn*. Time passed far too quickly!

We set off after a lazy start and met Robin at 9:30am at the campsite entrance. He was so keen to show us his area. Kindly took us boot shopping in Sheffield as I needed new boots as my old ones leaky. Found some more Meindls, called Meran. Feel fine, tempted by the lighter Ohio trainer type which fitted too. So did Fremington extra wide Altbergs. All size 6.

Eventually we reached Robin & Gwynn's house, a converted barn. Great to meet with 'old' friends again (from Settlingstones days). Washing, tent mending, shopping, then late to bed after a lovely meal and a wee dram!

We caught up with Dan and had a good phone chat. He seemed cheerful. Archie having chemo in Albury today and Dan taking the boys to the pub to his work where he is chef at the busy Jindera Hotel. More trips to Melbourne in June for them.

* We first met Robin & Gwynn in the late 70s when we lived at Settlingstones, Newbrough near Hexham.

Day 57.22/5 Blackwell to Edale

Fieldhead Campsite, Edale	12.1 miles
Warm, misty, drizzle, cleared afternoon	1767 ft

Robin and Gwynn sorted transport so Robin walked with us and Gwynn took our bags to Edale, meaning we walked with only a day sack – wonderful! Robin was our guide for the day so no route finding problems.
An excellent meal at the Ramblers, Edale and donations from the staff – many thanks for both!

Gwynn drove us back to Blackwell and with Robin and his dog Pip, we set off with light bags on the Limestone Way. Warm and cloudy start from Miller's Dale, Robin took us up lovely quiet dales, Monk's Dale, Peter Dale, Hay Dale – orchids, saxifrage and lots of birdsong!

Mist and cold as we climbed high, Bob & I didn't really want to bother with Mam Tor but it was good we did, as mist cleared and dramatic views back to the steep slopes of Mam Tor and a land slippage where the road is closed. I did a quick painting!

We headed down to the valley of Edale. Beyond, the land rose up forming the edge of the Pennines and start of the Pennine Way, the next stage of our journey north.

The start of the Pennine Way in the distance

We found the campsite and pitched up (now we are surrounded by big tents) and very chatty people. Oh well. We had a good meal at the Ramblers – chef and co gave us £10 when they saw Barney's card!

Looking forward to meeting Brian tomorrow (Brian is the coordinator of the Flatcoat Society Rescue, Rehome Scheme).

Section 4. The Pennines and the Cheviots

Edale to Jedburgh

2 nights wild camp, 1 bothy, 1 with friends, 1 pub and 16 nights campsites, 11 nights at home	**276.8 miles**
Pennine weather – often cool and damp but with sunny periods	**39876 ft**

A long and varied stretch up the 'Spine of England'.

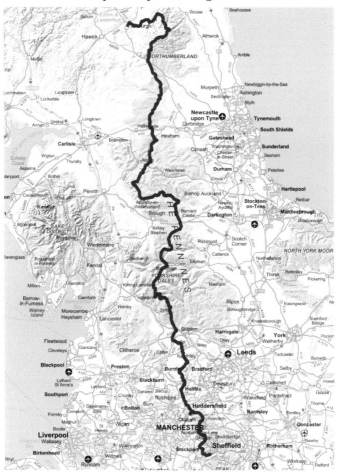

Unlike Andy Robinson's guide which takes an alternate route initially, we took the Pennine Way from the start at Edale. Our route then parted from the PW[*] at Garrigill, Cumbria where we made our own way north so we could stop off at home in Allendale, and pick up the PW again at Hadrian's Wall.

The PW route took us to Scotland from its beginnings at Edale in the Derbyshire Peak District, through parts of Yorkshire, Co Durham, Cumbria ending in North Northumberland and over the Border into Scotland at Kirk Yetholm. To finish this section of our walk we continued along St Cuthbert's Way to Jedburgh.

The Pennine Way follows high, upland ground, bleak, open moorland exposed to all weather, notorious for long boggy sections of often waterlogged peat (much of this now has large stone slabs laid down). Gritstone edges form the distinctive features of the South Pennines.

Stone slabs, common at both the start and end of the Way

In its southern section, the PW follows a narrow corridor of moorland sandwiched between conurbations, cities such as Manchester and Sheffield,

* Pennine Way

crossed east west by busy trunk roads we have to negotiate! Still a sense of solitude though, far from the madding crowd.

Further north, we marvelled at the dramatic limestone pavement area around Malham, the cove, gorge and Tarn, as we headed for the shapely hill of Pen-y-ghent, a steep climb when fully laden!

It's the end of May and I have to buy a winter hat and gloves at Horton in Ribblesdale, encountering freezing rain and gales as strong as those on the Cornish coast in March!

From Great Shunner Fell after Hawes, it was exciting to see 'our' Cross Fell in the distance (the highest hill in the Pennines), now we're returning to the familiar hills of home. Before that it is high exposed moorland walking, dropping down to dales and camping by swollen rivers, Swale, Tees. Here a great profusion of wild flowers, bluebells, globe flowers. We pass High Force waterfall and pitch tent by the Maize Beck just before the dramatic U shaped feature High Cup Nick, where despite the wind, I have to sketch!

High Cup Nick, North Pennines

Over to Cross Fell keeping to pathless high ground, to spend a freezing night just below the summit in Gregg's Hut bothy. Next day, buffeted down to Garrigill by gale force **June** winds! Here we left the Pennine Way as we took a direct northerly route across the heather moors home, to be greeted by friends and family.

A break at home to recover from 'summer' colds, rucksacks repacked and off North once more, crossing the river south Tyne and up to Hadrian's Wall re-joining the Pennine Way. Boggy high moorland, dark forests and booms from firing at the Otterburn Ministry of Defence ranges as we follow the Way up into Cheviot country.

I paint sleet showers on the long stretch of high ground between Byrness and Kirk Yetholm, the finish of the Pennine Way. It's the 21st June, the longest day!

Sunshine and showers 10pm

We are not finished though and now pick up The St Cuthbert's Way to Jedburgh, first over very green, grassy, flat topped, wide open hills contrasting with the dark broody Cheviot hills (or was it that the sun had come out at last!).

Into Scotland on St Cuthbert's Way

Day 58. 23/5 Edale to Crowdon

Crowden C&C Club Site	15.9 miles
Warm, grey, sunny later	2418 ft

Brian from Flat Coat Rehome & Rescue joined us, and as he knew the area well, acted as our guide – thanks Brian!

Up and off by 8am to meet Brian with his flatcoat at the campsite entrance.

Brian with one of his flatcoats – they're our guides for the day

He soon had us walking the original start of the Pennine Way – up a steep, rocky river bed – Grindsbrook. Barney climbed up like an old 'pro'. Once on the top, we reached the edge of Kinder Plateaux and the peat hags.

The infamous 'old' start to the PW across peat hags

Brian set his compass and led us over the peat hags directly to Kinder Downfall (a waterfall) where we met the new path again. We managed without getting too peaty! We carried on to Mill Hill where he turned back, bidding us good luck and farewell. Our route continued over Featherbed Moss on slabs, hard on feet, but better than bog!

We met a busy line of traffic, the A57 snaking along Snake Pass, after crossing the road, we stopped for a late lunch, looking at high land ahead, Shelf Moor, 621m.

Over the peat hags and heading for the Snake Pass

The Way steadily gained height following Devils Dyke all the way up to Bleaklow at 633m. Pity we missed the shapely Wain Stones, apparently the new path diverts away from them. Too tired by now to go back, and getting hot. The rest of route, a rocky downhill, heading west along Clough Edge all the way down to Longendale and reservoirs. We had to cross a dam and head through lovely woods to reach Crowdon C&C site.

Met by very friendly reception. Glad to get tent up. Lynden, Rob & Eileen also Lejogers here! (we met Lynden at Uttoxeter)

Card 8	Dear Jane, Back on hills again! From Edale we followed the old PW up onto the Kinder plateaux & across the peat hag area. Our guide was Brian from Flatcoat Rescue, who had 'given' us Barney!!
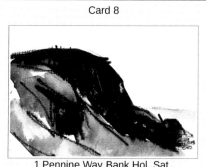 1 Pennine Way Bank Hol. Sat.	It's been a long hard day underfoot – lovely to be in Pennines, grouse, curlew & golden plover. All new area though, we are east of Manchester! Compass (internal one) points North & HOME!! A couple & single bloke doing LEJOG too, so we keep meeting up – might need to SOS you for more sketchbook by Middleton!! xxJxx

Day 59. 24/5 Crowden to Standedge

The Carriage Pub, Standedge	11.7 miles
Wet start, mist all way, cleared on arrival	2328 ft

Rain first thing and a steady climb up. Phone with flat battery so no pics!
Camped behind the pub at Standedge and had a Turkish meal!

Good sleep, quiet site, 6am start. Raining, so de-camped in the wet. Misty as we left and made our way along Pennine Way uphill alongside a stream, with steep rocky sections.

Bob seemed very puffed with weight of sack. I felt fine, up and up with stone slabs sections leading into the mist. Black Hill trig point reached, a white pillar on a bank of stone, used to be inaccessible because of deep bog!

Cold wind blowing, not at all May Bank Holiday like. Is it Saturday or Sunday! We

Pennine Way Walkers

plodded down hill crossing cleughs and water courses, aiming for a distant tea wagon we could see parked up in a lay-by! Joy – 2 mugs of hot sweet tea, bacon butty and cake. Just the best, whilst sitting with a view back to Black Hill.

We crossed a busy road, A635 onto Wessenden Moor and gained the Pennine Way again – good track leading down to Marsden, but we continued following the PW up and over hills to Black Moss reservoir. Met 4 Manchester lads who were so enthused by our walk / adventure. They spurred us on and told us of a shortcut to the pub campsite, so by 4pm we were pitching on a field behind the pub with the other Lejogers.

We spent hours in the pub – I had 3 pints of cider and a Turkish meal – wow! In the tent now, Bob and Barney fast asleep. Where tomorrow, I don't know. Can hear cars whizzing by on some cross Pennine route!

148

Day 60. 25/5 Standedge Edge to Jack Bridge

New Delight Inn, Jack Bridge	17.3 miles
Grey, cool wind. Sun later	2199 ft

A long stage of 18 miles as we get past the major conurbations. The M62 was busy and quite a culture shock!
We're camped near Hebden Bridge, again next to a pub – we could get used to this.

This is turning into a pub crawl!

We left in the cool grey of a morning, 8am, up the main road and onto PW north. We followed Standedge Ridge up on heather moor, with views down to green valleys and villages. A hum of traffic grew louder and after 2hrs from our starting, rows of cars and lorries on the M62 came into view...

M62 from the Pennine Way footbridge

Bizarre! We crossed over a bridge and it was a shock to see the speed and amount of traffic, we really have slowed to walking pace!

Another interesting edge next – Blackstone Edge, an escarpment of gritstone, climbers and boulderers about with their mattresses for falls!

Standedge Ridge

I stopped to paint (just once) Standedge:

The walk continued, paved slabs over moors, dropping to a pub, The White House. This time, we carried on, following a track alongside reservoirs in a cold NW wind.

Just Posing

Glad to find a sheltered nook for our lunch stop. The left side of my upper ankle hurting and swollen. It felt a long way, heading for the phallic monument on Stoodly Pike! Once reached, we climbed up dark stairs to see the view from the top, moors one way, Todmorden and verdant valleys the other. Not too far now, a slow gradual descent to sunshine and warmth in Hebden Bridge, crossing the canal, where barges and 'hippy' vans parked!

To reach the campsite we had to grit teeth and head steeply uphill again for an hour till we reached it at Jack Bridge. Tired, but next to a pub where we had large Yorkshire pud and Cumberland sausage for our tea along with a few pints!

A woman from Nairn made friends with Barney, she had 5 flatcoats! She also knew Rackwick, on Hoy, Orkney and Jack Rendall, our farmer friend. What a small world.

A day in the life of Barney on the trail

Barney's day starts when he gets up from lazing at the bottom of the tent – he sleeps at our feet, mostly on Jos's side where he has more room.

His breakfast is dished up and soon consumed, then it's back to bed while we have ours. Packing up follows and eventually he has to leave the tent as it's being taken down but not before Jos has anointed his paws with Mushers cream. The sight of the harness / panniers causes him to move some distance away as he doesn't much like it being fitted first thing even though it may be empty! A few minutes later however and he's forgotten it exists. From first awakening to leaving camp normally takes us about 2 hours – we're not fast!

We start walking with brief stops every 90 minutes or so. The morning proceeds and depending on the terrain, one or more stops may be taken before we have a longer break to eat lunch which Jos prepared earlier while I was cooking breakfast. If the site is right, she may be painting as well as eating and Barney would be asleep.

Similar for the afternoon until it's time to stop. When wild camping we aim to look for a place to pitch the tent by about 6pm and Barney knows we're finished for the day! When heading for a campsite it may be later. The tent is put up and Barney is more than ready for his evening food – after gulping it down he is looking to get into the tent and snooze! An hour or so later and he is up for a drink and a short wander with Jos before settling down for the night, 8:30 probably sees him fast asleep.

7pm and any passers by might hear the sound of the Archers from the tent while water is being boiled to make a cup of tea! I get our meal ready, normally a 3 course affair consisting of soup (cup-a-), main course (dehydrated packet meal) and sweet (cake with instant custard).

By about 9 or 9:30 we're probably also ready for bed, Jos is busy catching up in her diary, I could be updating the blog if we have internet access. We are both carrying Kindles and are reading if we can stay awake.

Throughout the day we see people on the trail and Barney brings a smile to almost everyone's face when they see him carrying his load! Visiting cards get handed out, photographs taken and Barney just stands and waits as he is used to it. He always enjoys any attention. We are now making a habit of noting down the comments made when people first see Barney carrying his load. Most we have heard before but we do occasionally get original ones like "Has he got his PJ's?"! Route finding includes Jos with the pre-printed OS maps for the day ahead and me with the mapping GPS and guide book descriptions to avoid us getting lost. If we pass a shop en route, we stop for goodies, also pubs / cafes for soft drinks or coffee but these are all few and far between on the route we are taking. That's about it – a simple life!

Day 61. 26/5 Hebden Bridge to Cowling

Winter House Farm, Cowling	14.7 miles
Sunny all day, cool on tops	2230 ft

Jack Bridge has an excellent shop near the Pennine Way so we had a coffee before we left.

Moorland walking along with reservoirs and then a break at Top Withins, the derelict farmhouse which is reputedly the source of inspiration for Emily Bronte's Wuthering Heights. One thing that is unusual is the footpath signs in the area, I don't know if it can be seen in the picture (following page) but they are in English and Japanese!

On then to Cowling and a campsite before 6 O'clock.

Lovely fine sunny start up the cobbled lanes to find the 'Aladdin's Cave' shop and it really was, a back room stuffed with stock. We had a coffee with almond cake outside and bought sandwiches, Parkin, bars and dog food – all shared out. Finally the walk began, first a good stride over moorland leading down to a reservoir via a cleugh (a deep sided stream valley). The route was next to 2 more reservoirs and we strode along with easy going. A steady uphill slope left the views behind us of yesterday's walk and now ahead lay Bronte country and Top Withins ruin, said to be the type of building featured in Wuthering Heights. An isolated, lonely farm house with a few trees, at the head of moorland. We sat in sun on a

Top Withins break (and sketch)

bench and I painted some Bronte views, though not stormy! A local man, a painter (from Haworth) chatted to us in his soft Yorkshire dialect.

Bronte country is popular with Japanese tourists, hence the footpath signs…

Footpath sign in English and Japanese

Off downhill to another reservoir, very warm out of the wind and uphill past Ponden Hall (also in Bronte book). The slog of the day was uphill through fields to gain height on the very north side of the River Worth Valley up onto Ickornshaw Moor. It was a brisk, cool, north wind and I felt quite buffeted. Great views to Pendle Hill west and unknown ones north. No sign of the conurbations not far away although we did see a power station on the Eastern skyline. Once off the windy moor we were nearly there.

Tired dog

Nice to be 'in' by 5-6ish – we dropped down to Cowling and a very busy A6068 to find the farm camp field, not far and not uphill! A basic and mucky shower but there was hot water. A church bell tolling every ¼ hour through the night, hens all round the tent and Mr Chook crowing in the early hours – peaceful spot!

Today the landscape looked very familiar, reminding me of Upper Teesdale and Weardale, very green in the valley but not huge grouse moor estates yet though.

Day 62. 27/5 Cowling to Gargrave

Eshton Road Caravan and Camp site, Gargrave	13 miles
Fine, dry, cloudy, cool and warm, rain by 4, heavy by 6pm	1702 ft

Moorland followed by lower ground and even a canal – who said the Pennine Way was all hills? It was up and down though.
Friends of Jos will be familiar with the trig. point picture!

We headed for the shop in Cowling on a very busy road. Glad to get off (we are very anti traffic now) and onto minor roads, lanes and paths up fields following PW signs.

Barney knows trig. points mean stop and sketch

Lothersdale looked very old with a mill chimney and buildings. Climbing up hill took us to a trig. point, Pinhaw, where I stopped to paint the hill to do with witches – PENDLE.*

Pendle Hill from Pinhaw Beacon

That was all I did today, on across the moors and down to the valley with a busy A56 to cross. We decided to carry on over sheep fields and rest by the Leeds – Liverpool canal.

Multi-level bridge

Looked very tranquil watching the slow barges – people on holiday.

* Infamous as the home of the Pendle Witches, tried and executed in 1612

156

We called in at cafe for a very welcome pot of tea, soup and a choc bar 'Rocky Road'!

Time for a snooze...

Then rejoining PW and in no time uphill and a view down to Gargrave (14 miles went quick). At the Co-Op, Bob took 2 attempts to buy the wrong 'instant' porridge – in the end I went in! We are now pitched on a site by the canal, rain hammering down on tent, waiting for it to ease so we can find the pub.

Another enjoyable day, a few awkward stiles and cattle grids with no dog gates made us cross. Otherwise a mix of field, sheep, stone walls, heather moor, villages with lovely gardens, canal, the Aire Gap and more sheep! Views of hills to come – hope weather ok – good to be cool for the dog.

Day 63. 28/5 Gargrave to Malham

Malham Campsite	7.1 miles
Cool, fine, dry	772 ft

After a wet night, a dry, cool sunny morning with strong wind on tops. Short walk. Up away from canals and onto Eshton Moor (sheep, cow fields – pasture) lovely views all round, ahead the limestone area above Malham. Dropped down to River Aire – lovely water bubbling along.

Limestone Country

We kept on downhill until village of Malham and all the limestone walls. First thing filter coffee and cream with jam scones!

Now pitched next to a stream, willow warblers calling, Malham Cove up the road. Will take a walk up there later. Nice to stop early, catch up with washing. Wish Bob would wash his smelly feet!

Malham Cove

Phones and Cameras

We carried smartphones and small cameras. Both required power not always readily available. This is a problem whenever trekking in the wild. Our cameras had replaceable batteries so carrying adequate spares was the obvious solution. Phones require a USB charging source however.

A second problem was posting pictures to Facebook and the blog which could only be done from Bob's phones. We were both using cameras which can be switched on only when needed in a few seconds and then powered down to conserve battery power. This was not so easy with phones which take a while to power up resulting in annoying waits. If the phones were left on then they needed regular recharging which wasn't always possible. The solution to this came when we arrived home part way through the trip. An OTG (On The Go) connection was used with a small USB card reader which allowed the memory cards in the cameras to be accessed directly from a phone. Now we could leave the phones switched off until needed for communications and use the cameras for the pictures.[*]

Day 64. 29/5 Rest Day

A day off, so we went for a walk! Only to Gordale Scar however.
Also tried the second of the two pubs in Malham, both dog friendly, excellent pubs!

Good to sleep in till 8am! Said 'bye to Mo the girl from Maine trekking alone. Rain, rain, no wind, so nice to put feet up!

After rain seemed to ease, we had a shop at a cafe for carbs. and walked to Janet's Foss through a lovely wooded stream valley with sun shafting through wild garlic.

On to rugged, grand Goredale Scar –I did some quick sketches as rain fell again and it was cold. Used pencil, mud and moss.

* Jos says she left all this to technical Bob.

160

We ended up in the Lister Arms for lovely meal – phew, I'm putting on weight, all these pub meals and beer, very nice though. After soup, I had polenta (slabs of something, tofu?), roasted veg and a tasty leafy salad. Pud was amazing, pink meringue, ice cream, strawberries and nuts! My favourite yet.[*]

Tomorrow we meet Tom & Miranda. Looking forward to that!

| 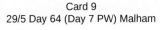Card 9
29/5 Day 64 (Day 7 PW) Malham

 | Dear Jane, Had a whole day off today at Malham. Slept in until 8am & in tent reading Wuthering Heights till 1pm!! had a short walk to see the Goredale Scar when rain stopped (& started!). Nice to be a tourist! Off again tomorrow to Horton in Ribblesdale via Pen-y-ghent. Tom & Miranda are coming out to meet us for wk end. We are getting near home. Could be next Sun 7/6 after camp in Galligill (Nenthall) – if you are home, maybe a lift up & walk back?? Be in touch. I got ur txt today! Really look forward to seeing my pals again! Haven't I been good keeping these up every Frid / or Sat!! This is with mud & moss! Lots Love Jos xxxx |

Day 65. 30/5 Malham to Horton in Ribblesdale

Holme Farm campsite, Horton in Ribblesdale	15.1 miles
Very cool wind, sun, cloud, dry all day	2983 ft

Quite a day....
Malham Cove first, not far from the campsite. This was followed by Malham Tarn and then onto Fountains Fell. The view north appeared, where we are heading. Next it was time for Pen-y-ghent and we were soon on the top.
On the way down we spotted Tom & Miranda making their way up. Great to see family. Onward together down to the campsite and who appeared but Joanna & Phil! A family gathering but no Ben who was busy working (aka FA Cup Final)

A very special day: half way! Started in good time and in sunshine, along the river to the Cove, then a steep climb up to the top.

---

[*] Readers will note that food becomes a very important part of long distance walkers lives and thoughts.

Malham Cove

Bob received a txt from Brian saying Flatcoat Retriever Society donating £1000! He got texting back, then chatting to a lady and went the wrong way – I put him back on track! We stopped to look at the top of the cove cliff edge.

Close to the edge

More sketching opportunity but had to press on, up the limestone

Limestone above the cove

gorge to lovely Malham Tarn – a good area to return to with our bikes. We continued on green sward, crossed a minor road, then track and uphill steadily to Fountains Fell.

Our next destination – Pen-y-ghent

Too cold to stop long but enjoyed great views of Pen-y-ghent and Ingleborough, the flat topped one.

When we got out of the wind behind a wall I had the chance to paint quick! Loved the edges.

The Path Up

Soon our turn to climb steeply up the edge of Pen-y-ghent although it wasn't too bad, again it was too cold to hang about.

Near the top of Pen-y-ghent

As we walked down the track we spotted Tom & Miranda! So lovely to see family again – they look very happy together too. They accompanied us to the campsite and we booked in – an old fella in a bizarre hut cum caravan!

When we came out, there were Joanna & Phil! Lovely surprise – really good to see them all, we went to the pub to celebrate and enjoy a family meal together. It was very busy tonight as a 3 Peak Challenge[*] on – a good atmosphere. Now back in our tents and van. We are near home now, could even see the Lakes today, yet still a week of walking. I love this slow pace of life.

Day 66. 31/5 Horton to Hardraw

Green Dragon Inn, Hardraw	15.7 miles
Very cold, wet and windy start then sun with heavy showers, gale force winds	1852 ft

A steady walk, first in rain then in wind to Hawes. The wind got so strong my rucksack cover was ripped off and disappeared!
After shopping in Hawes we moved onto the Green Dragon Inn at Hardraw – quite a pub. Included is the highest waterfall in England which you access by the pub.
Jos was disappointed that we missed an Irish traditional music session but we should be home for our next one at the Crown in Catton.

Writing this sat by a range with glowing fire! And just had lovely lamb shepherds pie! An **elemental day**, heavy rain all night, continuing as we got up, packed and said our goodbyes. We stopped at the Pen-y-ghent cafe in

* 3 Peak Challenge – Climbing Ingleborough, Pen-y-ghent and Whernside in one day.

Horton at opening time and stayed there an hour. Coffee, bacon butty and I bought a winter hat and waterproof gloves. Needed them today, the 31st May! Heavy rain to start and cold. When the sun came out, a strong wind got up – so strong we could hardly stand.

Heavy rain gets the streams flowing

Sketch of the day, back to Pen-y-ghent

Today felt quite a struggle, a long way and always battling the wind. Glad to reach Hawes in Wensleydale – just time for some shopping and then onto Hardraw via field paths in more wind.

Winter gear (Whernside and Ribblehead Viaduct in the distance)

Great to get tent up next to fast flowing stream – familiar spot to camp. Waterfall visit tomorrow.

Day 67. June 1ˢᵗ Hardraw to Keld

Rukin's campsite, Keld	11.5 miles
Cold dry start till 1pm wind and rain started	2325 ft

Over the highest hill yet on the trail, Great Shunner Fell. The weather was kind and we had good views of the hills north – our local ones, Cross Fell (highest in the Pennines) and Great Dunn Fell with the white 'golf ball' radar station. Down to Thwaite and onto Keld with the rain getting heavier as we progressed. Another great camping spot next to the river and another good pub for a meal; the Pennine Way is spoiling us.

A very cold night, heard rain in morning but dry on the whole to start. We were up 6am although didn't leave until 8:45.

We had a look at Hardraw Force, in good spate with all the rain.

Hardraw Force

Our route was up hill more or less straight-away – a steady plod up a track, onwards and upwards with fine views all round as clear with high cloud and not so windy. Some of the path was stone flagged. Didn't seem long (2 ½ hours), before we reached the stone wind shelter on top of Great Shunner Fell (716m). It felt quite a moment as familiar hills came into view: Cross Fell, Great Dunn Fell, Dufton Pike, Mickle Fell. Amazing to realise that we've walked back 'home' - well nearly.

Cross Fell from Great Shunner Fell

168

After leaving the top we headed downhill losing the wind and dropped down to Thwaite. A few women were planting out summer bedding, otherwise all very quiet. Kearton Tearooms didn't take dogs, so we didn't stop.

Bob slipped and jarred his ankle at a wall stile which made the rest of walk painful for him. We had some uphill out of Thwaite before a lovely track contouring around the hill, with the steep valley of Upper Swaledale below.

Further down, we walked through many fields, each with its own stone barn. Very distinctive birdsong today as we had moorland birds, snipe drumming, golden plover, peewits scolding us, and burbling curlew, different to the constant call of chiff chaff down south. Once back in woodland though, willow warbler calling cheerfully.

Feeling sleepy now, inside the tent on a farm site at Keld, a lovely spot by river. It's still raining and the river sounds very loud and close!

We went out in rain to find the pub. Friendly guy behind the bar and very dog friendly. When we came out after a good meal, the roads were flooding. The river was thundering past the tent and I hoped it wouldn't rise. Went to bed listening to the roar. I got up at 4am to check the tent, as I was imagining water lapping the tent and we'd be doomed, but all ok. Bit of sun to start.

Day 68. 2/6 Keld to Tan Hill Inn

Tan Hill Inn	4.5 miles
Very wet and windy, soaked through	973 ft

We decided to have a short day and stop at the Tan Hill Inn, the highest pub in the UK at 528m. More rain overnight which made the rivers very fast flowing. The pub is in new hands and being renovated but it didn't take much persuading to get us into a room for the night!

Shortest walk yet. Set off in rain, a very ploddy walk uphill over tussocky grass and moor, with rain sheeting in from the west and wet sheep gazing at us. Curlew, golden plover, snipe – calls of the moor.

Once over the rise of the hill, the Tan Hill Inn came into view and we dropped / dripped in!

Warm fire was too inviting to miss

We dried off by an open fire. After coffee, soup and beer we decided to ask if we could stop the night for a treat rather than camp. Fortunately a room was available. So here we are catching up on messages on phones as we sit on beds and another pub meal to look forward to.

From Tan Hill bedroom window

Batteries

Cameras, phones, head torches, air bed pump and GPS all require battery power – how were we to ensure they all worked when required?

The GPS, 1 camera and pump were straightforward using non rechargable AA and AAA lithium batteries. The GPS used 3 AA lithium batteries at a time which lasted 3 days – it alone required over 130 Lithium AA batteries for the whole trip:

144 Lithium AA batteries for the gps

Lithium batteries can't be sent through the post so they couldn't be distributed with other items which we posted ahead. Fortunately we were able to distribute a number of them by other means.

For the phones and 1 camera we required a backup charging source for when a mains supply was not available. Initially this was a fuel cell but this turned out to be not optimal and was replaced by a 16000mAh USB battery pack which covered our requirements when off grid. This was recharged when possible and then allowed us to recharge phones for several days.

Once into the highlands of Scotland, phone reception was much more variable so phones could be powered down thus saving batteries. My Fuji X10 camera used rechargable batteries so a number were carried to ensure it could be used for extended periods with no need to recharge.

Jos – More techie Bob speak!

172

Day 69. 3/6 Tan Hill to Middleton-in-Teesdale

Leekworth Caravan Park, Middleton-in-Teesdale	17 miles
Dry, got out sunny	1606 ft

We moved into our very own North Pennines AONB* and started to feel near home.
Moorland followed by farmland as we neared Middleton.
God's Bridge is a natural limestone slab over the River Greta and on the route.
As soon as we left the Pennine Way we saw Joanna and Phil turning up with our supplies so we had a lift to the campsite – much appreciated!

Dry, but a slow start as staff overslept, so breakfast a bit late! We didn't mind. We left at 9:30am and made good progress over bog and a damp track, heading downhill towards a busy A66. Saw Appleby caravans[†] on the road.

Stopped for a break at Gods Bridge – a huge limestone block makes the bridge, spanning the River Greta.

Gods Bridge

* Area of Outstanding Natural Beauty.
† Gypsies and Travellers heading for the annual Appleby Horse Fair. The biggest traditional Gypsy Fair in Europe with over a thousand caravans from all directions.

Time for a sketch:

then off for a long tramp after crossing the A66 by an underpass.

Uphill, and now a vast expanse of moorland. Once up at the 'brow', looking south, were the hills we'd walked over including Great Shunner Fell. To the north, lay Shacklesborough and Goldsborough, mesa like table topped hills above the Baldersdale reservoirs. There were Hannah's meadows[*] and on the skyline, Mickle Fell at 788m, Ministry of Defence land.

Landscape I've drawn, painted and walked, all becoming familiar again. We walked over to Grassholme reservoir, then more uphill through sheep fields, over stiles, till we were at last under Harter Fell with Middleton in view below.

[*] Hannah Hauxwell who farmed on her own, 1000ft up in Baldersdale, made famous by a TV documentary about her harsh existence especially in winter.

174

Day 70. 4/6 Middleton to Maize Beck

Maize beck wild camp	16.2 miles
Sunny all day	1938 ft

The weather turned good – shorts again.
A lovely walk along the Tees with Low Force, High Force and Cauldon Snout and we're on local paths.
Eventually camped just short of High Cup Nick.

Sitting outside tent 7:15pm and it's sunny and warm. Gentle sound of running water in Maize Beck. This morning we walked from Leekworth campsite, alongside the wide River Tees to rejoin the PW by the Middleton Mart.

Lovely walk through meadows, although lots of wall stiles slowed us down with taking Barney's pack off each time. He is good at assessing the stile and jumping!

Posing again

We soon had layers off, down to top and shorts! What a change in the weather from the last few wet, windy days.

We reached Low Force in full spate and carried on up to High Force, nearly 3 hours from Middleton – time for a break and a sketch.

On up river, linking up with a stretch friend Terri and I have walked to gain the Cronkley Fell trig. point. We rested in sun and out of wind behind a stone wall. Joanna and I once picnicked here and found the Teesdale gentian and birds eye primrose below us, on the riverbank.

On now to reach the awkward boulder section alongside the Maize Beck. At Falcon Clints, we spotted a kestrel and a ring ouzel. A fisherman we met said he'd seen a peregrine. The climb up beside Cauldron Snout seemed steep with rucksacks. Barney managed by big leaps up the rocky ledges – Rock dog! The last leg was a drag at first, uphill on a keepers hard gravel track, Pennine Way indeed! We were all relieved to step onto soft, wet, spongy grass when the stony track cut up to grouse butts on the hillside.

Cauldron Snout

At last alongside the Maize Beck in warm sunshine, 17 miles were telling, all ready to stop and put the tent up and make tea.

Now 9pm, I've been washing outside in the river, to the sound of snipe drumming, golden plover and continuous stream running noise – lovely and peaceful (until the early hours, see next day's diary). Wish I'd found a skinny dip place earlier. Poor Bob has caught a cold, let's hope it's over quickly.

Day 71. 5/6 Maize Beck to Greg's Hut

Greg's Hut Bothy, Cross Fell	10.9 miles
Good start, then cloud and gale on Cross Fell	2223 ft

A restless night due to an army helicopter – not sure what it was doing but it was close at 1am! See Jos was still up painting the view from the tent before 7am!

High Cup Nick is one of the highlights of the Pennine Way and although one of our local walks it was exciting to approach from a different direction.

We traversed moorland to avoid dropping down to Dufton and having then to climb all the way back up to Great Dun Fell. The weather closed in, not quite the warm sunny day previously forecast.

Eventually got to Greg's Hut and our first bothy of the trip.

I'm sitting on a bench at 9:10pm in a very cold Greg's Hut. Bright evening, sun bursting through the clouds, dark horizons. Thack Moor on skyline and other tops I've walked with friends Winky, Jane and alone, a very dramatic sky, wind blowing outside. Painting inspiration!

High Cup Nick

This morning when we woke, the day dawned light and promising, no wind, but soon greyed over. The weather changed as the day wore on, becoming dark after High Cup Nick – Familiar, stunning, wide U shaped space and vertical slabs of rock sides. Had to stop for a very rapid sketch, but very windy by now. We slowly made our way across pathless rough ground along Blackstone Edge. I led, Bob feeling rough with cold. When we reached a keeper track, I took a compass bearing for a point on the PW, as cloud's right down and wind up, bleak Pennines!

Little Dun Fell and Cross Fell

The cloud blew over and we reached the path and more solid ground – uphill trudge to first hill, wind increasing all the time and grey cloud on the top of Cross Fell. Sunshine west in the Eden valley and east below in Tyne / Tees river valley. Felt tempted to go down to Garrigill that way, but Bob seemed keen to keep high – quite a battle to get to top.

Cross Fell – Highest point of walk at 893m

I felt tired, then at the summit shelter, turned phone on and saw new pics of Archie, poor mite, losing his hair with chemo. Facebook on top of Cross Fell!

Feeling tired, because woken at midnight by a loud low helicopter – manoeuvers. Troops!* Bit unnerving – expected searchlights and soldiers bursting in, but after a long time of coming and going it buzzed away!

Sun still out now at 9:20pm. Shame we couldn't light a cosy fire, it really is freezing cold for June!

* We were pitched next to the M.O.D. range boundary.

Weird seeing Winky's Thack Moor and Fiend's Hill again. After we cooked our meal in the hut, skies cleared and now the light in the sky and on the hill is wonderful.

Thack Moor

I try to get the sharp outlines of hills with my paint against yellow sky, blue purple clouds. I had a go, what a remote high situation. Elemental. Glad we stopped, though next time we come, bring firelighters!

Bothy Life
We're in Greg's Hut, our local MBA bothy. Thanks to all the MBA members who donated after seeing the article in the latest newsletter.
MBA is the Mountain Bothies Association who maintain nearly 100 such huts around the country, mostly in Scotland.

Card 10	No words – hand delivered!
 5/6/15 Greg's Hut	

179

Day 72. 6/6 Gregg's Hut to Galligill

Haggs Bank Campsite, Galligill	10.3 miles
Gale	1008 ft

No blog pictures today – no battery.
A windy walk via Garrigill where we got a very welcome tray of coffee and biscuits from the Post office.
Campsite full of bikers, joined them for food and beer – great!
Home tomorrow...

Greg's Hut

Sun shone through the windows, very cold though when we left, very strong wind up, 2 hours down stony track to Garrigill and got delicious coffee from the PO on the village green. Bob struggling with his cold. What was lovely about Greg's Hut was getting all snug in my sleeping bag and feeling cosy and warm listening to wind roaring outside. What a place to work, live, sleep, in the past – brrr. This is June! Imagine the winter.

The wind really got up on our hike over Alston Moor – tiring staying upright! When we got to the campsite, found a meet of motor bike off road riders camping. Friendly lot, we struggled in the wind to put the tent up. Later we joined them for a BBQ indoors and **Allendale** beer!

Just rung Rosie as calling in hers tomorrow. Joanna & Ben are coming to walk home with us – finally!

Day 73. 7/6 Galligill to Home

Allendale – Home	13.5 miles
Sun, better day	2146 ft

Phil dropped Joanna and Ben off and took our sacks so we could all have an easier walk home.
Daffodils still to be seen – they were nearly over in Penzance when we started in March.
Eventually got to Burnlaw where Rosie & Gary who we last saw in Monmouth laid on afternoon tea in the garden. No pictures I'm afraid as Rosie's cake was too nice!
Then on to meet Barney's friends before the steep climb back to home.

Phil brought Jo & Ben over and took our big packs. With light day sacks, off we all went, straight up hill from Haggs Bank campsite. Nice gentle rise till up on Wellhope Moor with the big mine spoil heap and hut for the grouse shoot.

Family stroll home with Jo & Ben

Then down Middle Rigg to Rod Sutterby's garden, on down to Ninebanks bridge over the West Allen and warm sun! Lovely to see familiar local 'shapes' – woods, tracks, the Mohope Long Drag and we have our 2 'youngest' with us.

Up steps to Ninebanks church and Isaac's Tea Trail footpath, to join the track contouring round past Brian Summers 'untidy' farm, Mount Pleasant! Even a crashed aeroplane in yard! Crossed road past Val & Mick's, to Monks Wood, up to Monk Farm track and left turn on road to Burnlaw, to meet Sue, Gary, Rosie and tea and cake in their garden!

Close to home

Lovely to be cheered in

They walked with us down to Oakpool where more dear friends Cath, Christine, Ann, Noelle & Sue plus all their dogs were waiting for us!

Barney, eager to get home.

At last home, to my cats, plants and garden, so well looked after by our house sitters, Lucy and Batch.

Stuff in the garden

Meal in Crown in the evening and Irish music session with our friends! £40 collected. Phew.

Days 74 – 83 8/6 – 17/6

Next few days….

Bob still had a cough and cold, I had a sore throat. Bob thought it all started in the pub at Horton in Ribblesdale. He had an explosively coughy walker sat behind him as we ate and remembered thinking that's not good! A few days later and he was feeling the affect. I suppose we've been lucky so far, meeting people en-route is likely to introduce some bug or other and we've probably avoided most.

We used the time to good advantage however, made some kit changes and Barney enjoyed stretching out asleep for good parts of the day.

We had got into the routine of moving on from one day to the next with just the occasional rest day, so by the time we had adequately recovered we were both (not sure about Barney?) raring to go!

800 mile service

Barney was at the vets yesterday for a check-up MOT! Everything was fine. Hadrian Vets in Hexham are also collecting for Barney – many thanks!

Day 84. 18/6 Hudsriding to Stonehaugh

Stonehaugh campsite	14.2 miles
Grey, quite strong wets wind, cool, few showers and patches of sun	1767 ft

> *Away from home at last. The colds went on longer than we'd hoped so it was quite a relief to get away again.*
> *Walked along the River Allen, then crossed the South Tyne and up hill to meet Mick, Ann & Jane[*]. Mick & Jane walked with us while Ann had our sacks in her car so we could travel light.*
> *Across the Roman Wall and we rejoined our old friend the Pennine Way.*
> *On to Stonehaugh.*

Off again at last after 10 days at home recovering from cold and sore throats. I managed to get gardening done, carry on where Lucy and Mattie left off. Now it needs TLC until we return.

So today while Ann took our sacks by car to here (Stonehaugh campsite), we set off after 8:30am from home, I fed Jill's hens and off we go along the Staward road. Reached the station. 9:05am.

A local walk -the River Allen near Allenbanks

Quite quick going along the Peel and R. Allen to Allenbanks, there by 10:25 so roughly 2 hours from home, a short walk along A69, before crossing over,

* Mick & Ann we've known since Settlingstones days and Jane, the recipient of the postcards, and Jos had many art trips together, with Barney.

then a track uphill, north up to Thorngrafton Common, and steeply up to join Stanegate, where Mick, Ann and Jane were awaiting at 11:30.

After us having a bite to eat, we crossed road to follow track and footpath past Crindle Dykes up to the Military road. Crossed it and headed up to the Wall to meet the Pennine Way again.

Our journey beginning again, the Pennine Way heading north of the Wall over remote boggy land and into dark forest. To the east, Queens and Kings Crags, Sewingshields.

Familiar territory near Hadrian's Wall

Quite a strong, cool wind from the west, it rained just enough to put our wet gear on. Not for long though, it got warm on the forest tracks.

It wasn't a monotonous route, but quite varied, with some open land, the Willow Bog bonsai place came in view, a lovely mass of cotton grass on one open heath. Great to have company too.

The final footpath led us through pine needles of the dark forest, straight out to the campsite where Ann was waiting with our sacks!

Thanks and goodbyes said after putting the tent up, and here we are again, Bob's smelly feet, smelly dog and me! Our few possessions by our sides, porch ends, pockets.

A wind generator whirrs, wind in trees, birdsong, and sheep calling.

Good to be back.

The Stonehaugh Totem Poles

Day 85. 19/6 Stonehaugh to Bellingham

Demesne Farm campsite, Bellingham	8.2 miles
Grey, cool, wind dropped, warm in Bellingham	725 ft

A short day with full sacks. Went past Shitlington Crags (spelling is correct), then crossed the North Tyne to enter Bellingham.

Short day! In Bellingham just after 1pm.

Left at 9am. Pleasant walking, just enough with full sacks again. Only met one person, a female vicar. We walked on bridle path through forest and open hill to drop down to the Warksburn, a limestone valley and up the other side to Horneystead Farm, where inviting friendly signs for tea and coffee.

We carried on, hoping to find Kim Lewis[*] at home in her remote cottage, but all shut up. Tracks through pasture took us past the farm where Sheena from Muck[†] now lives. I flagged down the approaching car, in case it was her, it was the lady vicar again, who took our regards. Leaving the Muck like single track road, the PW took fields where I stopped to paint forest on the skyline,

---

[*] Another artist friend and author of children's books.
[†] Island of Muck where Jos has stayed many times to paint.

green fields and trees and Houxty Burn valley. All lush and lots of sheep and lambs.

Down to the burn to cross by a footbridge and up to Shitlington Hall Farm, continuing uphill to Keith Turnbull's old place, Shitlington Crags.

North to Ealingham Common

What a panoramic view Keith had before he met his demise[*].

Shitlington Crags

More up hill to a mast on Ealingham Common where below in the North Tyne Valley, lay Bellingham – good to see our destination so soon!

*Marmalade making with a faulty gas cooker.

188

We carried on downhill to tracks by the road, then river to find the campsite on Demesne Farm. Here we are, very quiet, tent up, sandwiches and cups of tea inside.

Raining lightly, blackbird singing.

Day 86. 20/6 Bellingham to Byrness

Border Forest Holiday Park, Cottonshopeburnfoot	14.2 miles
Warm, drizzle, no wind, cloud. sun end of day, still, very sunny and midgey	1849 ft

A classic Northumberland day – moorland and forest, rain, sunshine and midges!

Long day – thought it would be. Off by 9am in almost rain, warm and muggy. We gained height quickly, up by road and farm track and would've had a view back to our hills and Cross Fell if they'd been clear.

Cyclone Challenge Sportive

Once up, the going was soft and easy – quite dry. We crossed a minor road and Bob was delighted at seeing lots of cyclists, even an Allen Valley Velo shirt. He got quite animated!

The weather picked up after our first break, then a light shower made Bob a bit fed up. He'll have to chill, a bit up tight? Tired maybe? We warmed up by the time we had lunch, coats off and sun out.

Cheviot from Brownrigg Head

I painted from a high point by a fence – Brownrigg Head, with forest one side, moorland the other. Great views N E to West Woodburn and up to the Cheviot and range of hills we follow tomorrow.

Sunshine lit up patches of land with cloud shadows travelling across hills. We heard a loud bang from the military ranges at Otterburn and watched a big plume of smoke at the ranges!

Entering forest was pleasant at first, soft, boggy, but when a track started, it was hard on body and soul, it seemed a very long track.

Grit teeth. Very glad when little stream appeared then lovely walking by the River Rede, and so relieved when campsite reached. Very tired and probably dehydrated. Alex, the girl who was on Bellingham site is here, also doing Lejog but much faster!

Quiet site and Barney waiting for his tea

Lovely hot shower – especially on sore shoulder.

Card 11 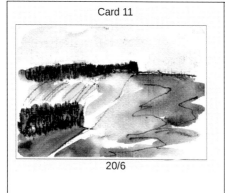 20/6	Now at Byrness, well Cottonhopeburnfoot actually! Camping by Rede. Long walk from Bellingham today up over open moorland. Grey start otherwise would have seen our N. Pennines – Cold Fell etc, but cleared later so lovely hills – Cheviot ridge all in view & lots of cloud shadows. Army busy too, 'bombing' - Great you walked with us to see us off – back into the swing of it again, look forward to 'wild camp' on Windy Ghyle or somewhere tomorrow 21st! Hope it's sunny like tonight. FIRST MIDGES now breeze dropped. So light to go to bed! Txt wot no. card this is!! lots Love xx Jos

Midges out in force!

Day 87. 21/6 Byrness to Clennel Street

Clennel Street wild camp	15 miles
Sunny start, wind, rain, SLEET. Evening breezy, sun and rain	2770 ft

> *High level walking, much of it alongside the Border fence with the sound of gunfire from across the valley. We passed a number of troops, probably heading towards the battle, as the Pennine Way is next to the Otterburn Ranges.*
> *Finally camped in England for the last time this trip, pitched next to the Border fence.*

Sunny start as we left camp by 8:20am and walked in woods by the River Rede. Near Byrness we came up to a little church with lights on and a few cars.

The PW was across the A68, a steepish climb straight up through forest, until a scramble up big sandstone edge boulders.

Coquet Head, into Scotland, briefly

We needed all our wet weather gear on as a fresh wind and showers. Lovely and exhilarating to be on the rounded Cheviot ridge with views west into

Scotland, east, Northumberland hills and cloud to the south. We had a break later where the Coquet rises and I sketched the valley running east.

Up the Coquet – Thirl Moor Edge from Coquet Head

Arms fire coming from MOD close by and military vehicles in distance.

Pennine Way meets army range

We walked to a valley at Chew Green where Romans camped, then uphill to rejoin the tops with purple clouds and heavy rain coming from the west as we made for a mountain shelter.

We passed 15-20 soldiers on the path, all carrying big sacks and rifles, Belgians, a friendly lot.

When we reached the hut, more piled out as we made to go in and they left us to it. We brewed a hot coffee and watched hail cover the ground (21st June). We were just in time and sheltered from the worst of the storm while having lunch. I did 2 paintings from the steps, moody skies and hills – in my element!

Passing Sleet Storm

Sunshine broke through and wind increased as we set off again.

Both tiring by the end as we plodded up the biggest hill of the day, Windy Gyle. From the summit, far reaching views north west to hills and lowlands where we'll walk later and east, very soft, spongy green interlocking spurs down to Barrowburn.

Cheviot in the distance

We met a man and his dog!

Then, where to camp? On downhill, stepping on slabs of stone avoiding peat bog. We stopped at a crossing point, Clennell Street, an old drove track, coming up from the valley and over the tops.

We found a flattish area to pitch, quite windy, so tied guys to the Border fence!

Bob had to go and seek water – I felt drained but revived after sugary tea and then food.

West into Scotland from Border Fence wildcamp

The light at 9-10pm was beautiful, soft lemon and greys – sun and rain at same time, what an isolated position for a camp on the longest day – 21/6. I had a go at painting before bed. Now tent flapping, rain, Bob and dog snoring and light going with clouds at 10:30pm.

Day 88. 22/6 Clennel Street to Town Yetholm

Overnight with John & Angie, Town Yetholm	12.8 miles
Cold (winter hat), wet, fog all day until end	1729 ft

A wet walk, so we missed most of the views but two big occasions, we've walked out of England and finished the Pennine Way.
After getting our customary free half pint in the pub at Kirk Yetholm we are now staying with friends Angie and John* at Town Yetholm. A good meal and the luxury of a bed tonight – thanks!

Left to Scotland, straight on to Cheviot

A wet start, up in clouds, and like it all day. Felt bit tired and slow on the uphill – not very uplifting when no view and all you can see is the path of stone slabs bordered by heather and bog.

We got to the turn off (Cheviot is one way, Scotland the other) after an hour or so and began heading west, into the wind and wet. At the mountain hut, good to brew coffee just as rain really came down but still a mist. Then up the Schil and no views until we took the old lower Pennine Way into a green valley.

* Angie & John used to live next door to Rosie & Gary.

196

Too damp and cold to sketch, so we pressed on, with a steep tarmac hill to finish – taking us to KIRK YETHOLM and straight to the Border Pub and a free ½ pint!

The official end of the Pennine Way

Had another pint and then walked to John & Angie's lovely cottage at Town Yetholm, with hills out the window. Very nice evening meal and chat but it's not sunk in that we've achieved walking all the way up England to reach Scotland. Just taking it in our stride, day by day!

PS Found another lump on Barney – chest area, hmm, tick I hope.

Day 89. 23/6 Kirk Yetholm to Jedburgh

Jedburgh C&C Site	18 miles
Cloud, warm, sun, hot – shorts. Cool evening, no midges	2333 ft

One of the few days where we finished south of where we started.
We followed St Cuthbert's Way, but the way-marked route has changed from when our maps were produced so we were on a magical mystery tour. Eventually got to Jedburgh 18.5 miles later.

Nice relaxed start with J & A, over breakfast, so didn't leave them till 9ish. After the shop at Town Yetholm, it was 10am when we set off along the river meadows, heading west. A short stretch of road walking before a track up to the green hills, with quite steep ups! Lovely views all round, down to river valleys and back up to dark cloudy Cheviot. The green bumpy hills here didn't feel bleak like the Pennine heather clad tops, or was it just the sunshine?

Different waymarkers now we have left the Pennine Way

All very quiet, although we met a few walkers coming from Jedburgh direction, so we gave them Barney cards. We dropped down to the village of Morebattle where we stopped for orange outside the pub and got chatting to a Corbridge taxi driver who gave us £5 and the pub gave us £10!

The sun was out and HOT as we plodded on tarmac. Barney was very slow and we had to stop to rest in shade and that was 2:30-3pm. Bob took his bags and he livened up!

We took tracks signed St. Cuthbert's Way and it went on forever, round fields, through woods – a mystery tour as not on our map! Very tired by the end as we finally dropped down to the A68, with sore feet. C&C Campsite by the river just after a garage where I bought bread and goodies, luckily we had a camp meal – phew.

Late now 11pm after shower but still light, River Jedwater bubbling along.

Section 4 finished

All of Scotland lies ahead!

GPS

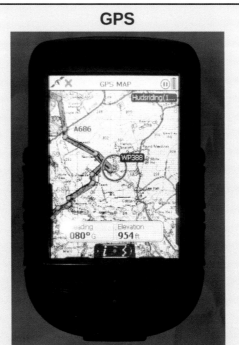

My SatMap GPS, preloaded with the entire route provided an instant method of determining our location along with an indication of our surroundings. It however required over 130 AA lithium batteries to keep it operational through the whole trip. Although the SatMap takes rechargeable Lithium – Ion batteries we couldn't rely on being able to recharge them due to the remoteness of our route.

Our SatMap has the 1:50000 Ordnance Survey map installed which matched the printed maps which we carried. In some places the 1:25000 would have been useful as it includes walls and fences but generally 1:50000 was fine.

Maps, guidebooks and batteries were sent ahead to reduce the daily load although due to posting restrictions for lithium batteries I did carry large numbers at times.

Jos carried the days printed maps in a waterproof cover and I had the GPS always at hand. The guidebooks were used as required.

The combination of printed map and GPS works well – Jos with the days map could see the general flow of the route and details on surroundings, I managed the fine detail with the more limited map view on the GPS.

We also carried a spare, small gps and traditional compasses in case of problems.

Section 5. Southern Scotland and into the Highlands

Jedburgh to Fort William

7 nights wild camp, 2 with friends, 1 in bothy and 10 in campsites	235.4 miles
Mixed weather, cool and often wet in hills, hot and sunny in lowlands	26618 ft

The whole of Scotland now lies before us, exciting as looking forward to walking and camping in our beloved high mountains again, still not thinking about the end though.

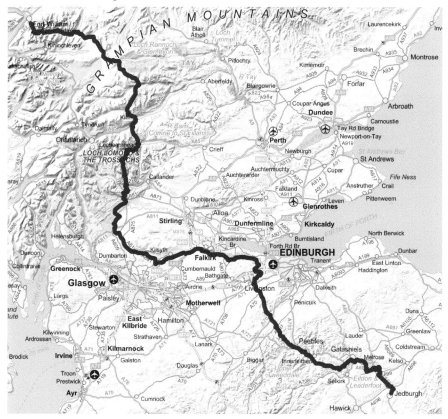

A long stage of great contrast from pastoral Border rivers and hills to the lowlands, The Central Belt and back up to high uninhabited mountain country. From Jedburgh, lush meadows and river paths walking alongside the Tweed, to hike over the Eildon hills to the historic town of Melrose. We walk over more hills on the Southern Upland Way looking down on the river Tweed from our vantage point overnighting in a wooden bothy at Minchmoor.

View from Minch Moor Bothy

A wild camp on the slopes of the Pentland hills from which we have extensive views down to The Forth and Clyde lowlands, Edinburgh, and Arthur's seat. Our route below, was to thread its way between the outskirts of Edinburgh and Glasgow on very quiet canal tow-paths, avoiding busy conurbations and motorways not far away! The sun even shone, even a mini heatwave.

Leaving the canal at Kirkintilloch, we began to head for the hills and glens following our own route – The Wet 'n Wild Way. It rained every day as we walked, pitching the tent by swollen rivers, on boggy bealachs (mountain passes). I was in my element now with the weather and landscape more challenging, painting sometimes from the shelter of the tent pitched in remote spots.

From tent on Rannoch Moor

Often over pathless terrain we made our way to Killin in Perthshire via Aberfoyle and the Trossachs. Then onwards north to Glen Lyon, Bridge of Balgie and Rannoch moor, eventually reaching Fort William by the wilds of Glen Nevis.

On the track down to Loch Ossian Youth Hostel

Here we found mountain rescue teams searching for 2 missing walkers where the waters of the Nevis and Steall Falls thundered down in torrential rain. Shops and hot showers for us on a campsite beneath Ben Nevis.

Day 90. 24/6 Jedburgh to Melrose

Melrose Gibson Park Caravan Site	19.3 miles
Muggy, grey, warm only spatter of rain	1973 ft

A long day of over 20 miles through the Borders.
Dere St. (Roman road) took us to St. Boswells where we followed the River Tweed for a number of miles.
The sting in the tail was the climb over the Eildon Hills to get to Melrose. The cloud came down as we neared the climb so no pictures of the view.
Arrived at nearly 9pm so fish & chips for all of us.

Ouch, too long, but we made it. Set off relaxed but late as we were tired from yesterday. So it was 10am by the time we departed after a shop in the garage. A road walk until crossing the A68, then very pleasant, alongside the River Teviot where I had the chance to do the one sketch of the day...

River Teviot

Walking in Monteviot House Estate through lovely woodland took a while as very convoluted – we didn't stop at the Harestanes visitor centre.

Once away from the estate, we picked up Dere Street, a very straight path through grassland and large trees. On a ridge where we stopped for a sandwich, the Battle of Ancrum Moor took place, when the English were slaughtered after they'd raided Melrose! Hard to imagine, very peaceful now, yellow hammers calling.

After rejoining the A68 nearby – we swung east (more road) and caught the edge of St. Boswells. Bob wanted to take a short cut, but I wanted to follow St. Cuthbert's Way all round the River Tweed. Lots of steps and bends, until

204

a golf area – met a nice woman from Broughty Ferry near Forfar where guide dogs are trained – she gave us £10.

By now, time getting on, 5pm and we had long way to go – Newton St Boswells, then more back roads. All the while the Eildon Hills which had been clear all day, now had cloud drifting across them and we had to get over the saddle. We would have camped if we had rations, a man did offer us water but we had to keep going, so finally up the hills on easy tracks – not that bad. Pity about the view. We just saw Melrose below, glad to get here, find fish & chips, down them, get dog food and porridge from Co-Op, and find campsite. I showered phew – feet tingling.

Fish and chips for all

25/6 Melrose rest Day

Reading, washing (in a machine) lunch in pub, wander round town, abbey, bookshops, more reading, lots of texting and evening meal in pub. Muggy warm night.

£20 collected in pub

Day 92. 26/6 Melrose to Minch Moor

Minch Moor Bothy	17.5 miles
Muggy, very warm, light rain, evening sun	3346 ft

A long day which included the 3 Brethren and then some fine high level walking. Barney met a fellow dog collecting for Guide Dogs! Barney accepts donations online at www.JustGiving.com/BarneysLongWalk

I'm on a bunk, a wooden platform, in a wooden hut in a forest. Thrush still singing outside, 10pm. Lovely view from the verandah down to the River Tweed meandering in evening light with hills all round. Today was hard. First, because we read a message from Sal on Archie's Story how he's to have an 'op in the next 3 weeks to hopefully remove cancer – phew, a bit scary and will need plastic surgery. Dan later says a bit of skull to remove – what a delicate op – but they are so good. We still don't know whether they want us over; we need a proper chat. So I had them on my mind, my sack felt too heavy and it was hard hot work. However it was a nice start once alongside the Tweed with quite a few dog walkers about.

Doesn't smell like a dog...

We were away by 9am and in at 7pm so a 10 hour day! The worst was crossing a river bridge and walking next to the busy A7. Not for long though, our route away and up hills, contouring round the forested Gala Hill, near Galashiels, up onto pasture, before leading us downhill to the Tweed again. A track led past homes and back into forest for a steady uphill. We stopped for lunch, then continued on up, till we were out of the trees and at the 3 Brethren. Here we found a trig. point and 3 large cairns, where we sheltered and I sketched the Eildons, very quickly:

Still a long way to go, but at least we were on the high level with extensive views, even though cloud, but hilltops not covered luckily, it could have been driving rain.

I got slow as stiff hips and Bob's feet hurt, at one point I felt tears as I felt low and slow! But didn't moan and a slow plod means you get there in the end. We were on an old drove road, so much history, more battles.

At last we found a trickle of water and filled up our bottles, then the bothy came in sight, a wooden hut with a balcony and no-one in, except a resident mouse!

Minch Moor Bothy, now sadly closed

I sat outside enjoying the view, gradually we revived with tea and a meal. A little mouse is on the floor, don't get them in the tent! 18 miles is too long. I did some painting of the light on the Tweed below.

Card 12	Now sitting outside Minch Moor bothy – wooden in forest, with lovely view of R. Tweed west, sun just going down. Lots birds singing – maybe owl later! Long day again, felt tired even after day off, so muggy, until we got up on the tops, where fresher. Worrying about little Archie, now due a face op – to try & remove all the tumour. Will need plastic surgery too – in good hands tho. We wait to chat to Dan, re whether they need us now or later – Dear me – poor things. Well it's nearly time to go inside, blow beds up, & light a night light – Barney's asleep after 18 miles – lovely countryside, v. quiet – on S, Upland Way. These are our last view of the Eldons which we crossed 2 days ago. Did it from the 3 Brthren stones on a hill top! Xxx
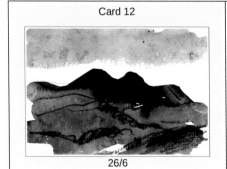 26/6	Happy birthday Monday!! xx

Day 93. 27/6 Minch Moor to Meldon Burn

Noisy 'wild' camp	13.8 miles
Warm, sunshine. No rain all day	1988 ft

Decided to shorten the stage and camp at Meldon Burn but it turned out to be a weekend campsite for drinkers etc. - not good as you may be able to see from one of the pictures showing rubbish left around.

15 miles, not too bad.

Nice sunny start at the bothy, phoned Dan. Also got a call from Joanna, bizarre really when you feel so far away from everything – but communications means we can talk to Dan. Sounds like they are in need of family support. It's back at the forefront now, giving up the walk to go out to help; Bob's adamant that it's the right thing to do, that the walk is just a holiday and not priority like they are. But he'll still feel disappointed at not achieving the whole walk in one go, but hey, the dog could've been ill, we could.

Anyway, today we had a minor road from Innerleithen to Peebles – the route 'avoided' it but took us up, down and round gravel tracks in the forest, we still came down to the road and had, I don't know, 3 or 4 miles to plod in SUN! Very hard on feet by the time we reached Peebles.

Looking back to Peebles

A church fete in a park saved the day with a mug of tea and cream scone for £2! Spent time doing a shop before heading out of town, then uphill to fresher air, with lovely views of valleys and distant hill tops – could've painted but we keep going.

On the Meldon Hills

Once over a wall (good old Barney scrabbled up) we were on the Meldon Hills. Looking down to the Meldon Burn we saw cars with tents where we intended to wild camp. It was a mini Glen Etive – young lads, cars, beers and fire, can hear them now. Why do they "F***ing" shout at each other so much! Now the beat of music from car – grrr... Pretend I'm at Glastonbury. Oh it didn't rain today!

Meldon Burn, rubbish scattered everywhere

Day 94. 28/6 Meldon Burn to Cairn Muir

Wild camp by Ravendean Burn	14.1 miles
Rain to start, warm, light showers, sun and dry evening	2223 ft

We made our way to the Pentlands via West Linton. Met nobody all day then 3 in the space of an hour. First we met a flatcoat owner and Barney had a girlfriend! Then we met the Laird's mother who previously had a flatcoat and suggested a good spot to camp. Finally we were invited in for a cup of tea by Caroline who lives next to the Drove Road we were following. A great afternoon.

In tent, 8:30pm. Bob cooking rice, murmur of stream or burn rather, with skylarks singing. Slight wind in tent fabric.

This morning, rain fell which eased off as we packed up, but the tent was all soaked for Bob to carry. Soon we were taking top coats off as we walked uphill in the forest, a little confusing regarding route description and changes, so we faffed around a bit before hitting the right path around Harehope Hill. Out on the hill, then down to the Flemington Burn where we stopped for a rest and painting.

Sitting on old drove road to Ramannobridge above Flemington Burn

We were on an old drove road from Peebles to Romanobridge. All lush green, soft grass, nice to stride on – imagine the herds of cattle with drovers in the past. The sun came out as we reached Romano House, where we had lunch on the grass before a boring long 3 mile road walk to West Linton, but fortunately in a cool breeze. Lo and behold, a tea shop with outdoor garden for good pot of tea and scones, what a reward after the road. Out of West Linton, a small village with Co-op, pub / hotel along with a few other shops, it was good easy walking up a track out of town, then a green trod following the Lyne Water up to Baddinsgill House and reservoir.

Wet dogs

We met a man out walking with a 3 year old flatcoat, Peppa, and fell in step with him. He was interested to hear our route and we talked flatcoats while we let Barney off to have a play. Peppa dived into water like our previous flatcoat, Sam, used to. Her owner showed us a pleasant, flat, grassy sheltered spot to camp by the river but it was only 5pm so we thought we'd continue for another hour and get higher up the hill. Good we did as next person we met was an old lady / ex Mrs Laird of the estate, who had owned a flatcoat and was very taken with Barney's bags!

Another woman, Caroline, joined us, and invited us into her cottage for the loo and a cuppa tea. Lovely red haired woman, ex paediatric nurse, singer, musician and now baby carer for a friend in high places – so they travel a lot – Australia. Lots to talk about including another friend, a niece of George Mackay Brown, the Orcadian author.

It was 6:30pm by the time we left and set off refreshed, following the drove track up hill, so nearly 7:30 when we pitched the tent here by the Ravendean Burn. A curlew calling overhead now, sheep baaing and still skylarks. A peaceful night tonight and wind light. I painted as the light went.

No contact with Dan today – both put off thinking about the inevitable, possibly needs to sink in, digest before decisions etc.

Day 95. 29/6 Cairn Muir to West Clifton

Linwater Caravan Park, West Clifton	12.5 miles
Rain to start, grey, warm	927 ft

Finally left the Borders after nearly a week's walking as we passed over Cauldstane Slap. Then onto Corston Hill with great views all round including Edinburgh.
Countryside walking even though we're now away from the hills. A nice campsite for the night after 3 nights wild camping.

Rain on tent in morning AGAIN!

Cauldstane Slap and we leave the Pentland Hills

Packed up and over Cauldstane Slap and down the north side, another layer of country ahead. Some flat fields of cows and sheep, then a stop by the Waters of Leith to make phone calls. Rang Dan in Melbourne, with the boys, Archie in hospital with another infection. He told us Sally's mum who lives in the USA, probably going out to help first. Relief yet torn, we want to see them and help, but want to stay and finish the walk. We also had a guide dog worker to ring and make arrangements to meet up. Gave me a headache with the effort.

On with the walk, up the small Corston hill with a trig. point and huge views: south, the long line of Pentland Hills, east, the Edinburgh skyline with Arthur's Seat very prominent and north, the built up Central Belt, but still lots of green.

We descended to a quiet road and had to cross a busy one, then into woodland. We got a bit lost 'off track'. Reached Mid Calder, and shopped. Next a river path and sets of bridges in the Almond Valley, all lovely and peaceful. Got to campsite eventually to be met by friendly Nikki from Guide Dogs with a pup, to arrange tomorrow's get together with puppy walkers. The very friendly site lady wouldn't let me pay.

Both irritable. Tired with the Oz worry and Guide Dogs 'organising'.

Day 96. 30/6, West Clifton to Linlithgow

Loch Farm campsite, Linlithgow	12.1 miles
Warm, sunny	611 ft

A canal day followed by a meeting with puppy walkers arranged by local Guide Dog organiser Nikki.

Flat towpath walking and it's hot and sunny again

Canal walk was OK, not many birds, sludge brown water and lots of trees which were good shade, when the sun came out it got very hot – Barney managed.

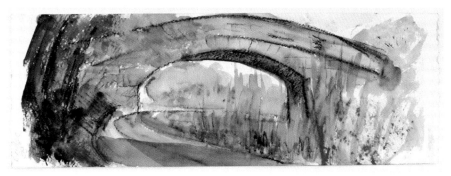

Union Canal

One thing of interest though…

We stopped for rests, then in no time met Nikki with dog Micky and walked on to Linlithgow.

Welcoming party from Guide Dogs – Nikki and dog Micky

A tempting tea place by the canal, but Nikki took us to dump our sacks in her car and buy tea at a pavement cafe in centre of town. 2 pup walkers arrived and we continued to the castle park at Linlithgow Palace where more turned up. 7 'pups'in all, 3 or 4 months to 14 months. All 'retired' people enjoying the challenge. A woman says it becomes addictive.

Barney laid down on the grass most of the time, too tired to care! Nice to chat and learn a bit more about the Guide Dog process[*].

---

* Puppy Walkers (now called Puppy Raisers), are volunteers who take on a puppy for a year or more. They play a vital role in the early socialisation and education of a guide dog. It takes a lot of time and commitment.

Quite a welcome from Scottish Guide Dogs puppy walkers

Nikki drove us to the campsite and is picking us up tomorrow. A very dedicated, proactive young woman. We pitched between parked up old caravans and campervans, nearby M9 traffic whizzing along. We do have some contrasting nights! Had to walk down town to buy haggis and chips.

Linlithgow Loch and Castle

Nice to eat on a bench by the loch then swift ½ of 'not' cask ale. Bob sniffed at that. I even had a go at sketching a castle.

Good shower, then bed, birds singing all night and it felt very warm!

Guide Dogs and Dogs Unite!

Dogs Unite* is a fund raising section of Guide Dogs. It arranges and supports sponsored dog walks in order that dog owners can raise money for the charity. We initially approached Guide Dogs about using our (Barney's) End to End walk to raise money, and made contact with Lorraine at Dogs Unite who had just joined the organisation.

Photo by: Dean Sawyer

Photographs of Barney were taken just before we started, publicity produced and sometime later, Dogs Unit initiated 'Match a Mile for Barney'. This was a novel scheme, inviting dog owners to make their own sponsored walks, matching a mile against Barney's achievement. More than a thousand signed up with over 800 raising £35 or more each, in some cases, much more.

Money raised for Guide Dogs:
* En Route: £789.60
* From Flatcoat Retriever Society: £1400
* Other Collections / Donations (at least): £832.04
* JustGiving: £7321.84
* Match a Mile for Barney (greater than): £22000
Total: Over £32000!

* Dogs Unite no longer exists as a separate fund raising section of Guide Dogs

218

Day 97. 1/7 Linlithgow to the Falkirk Wheel

Staying with John & Penny near Stirling	11.8 miles
Hot when sun out	705 ft

Another day walking a canal towpath and it was hot.
The highlights were the Falkirk tunnel and then the Falkirk Wheel.
The tunnel is over 600m long and built only in order that the landowner didn't see the canal!
The wheel is spectacular taking boats up / down from one canal to another and replaced the many original locks which were filled in 50 years ago. It takes only a very small amount of power to operate as it uses the weight of one arm to lift the other.
Our friends John & Penny* arrived soon followed by Fiona from Guide Dogs.
We are staying with John & Penny for the next two nights so they took the opportunity to take us to see the Kelpies – giant horse sculptures. Very impressive.

Up at 6am and Nikki picked us up on the dot of 8. Already t-shirt weather! We did a quick shop in Sainsburys for lunch, then set off along the canal from where left off yesterday. Barney a bit stiff but loosened up. Hot when sun out, not much shade. Didn't meet people to talk to as no bags on dog to attract attention.

Nice to walk free of sacks, Nikki had them in her car.

Grangemouth Refinery just a few miles away

Canal walking, a pleasant way to pass through the busy industrial belt and all those motorways. Very peaceful walking alongside the still brown water and tree lined bank. It just took a while.

* We met John & Penny in the Himalayas, on a trek to Kanchenjunga Base Camps. They live near Stirling.

The Falkirk Tunnel

The tunnels were good and cool.

When we got to the Falkirk Wheel, Nikki was there to show us the amazing structure:

The Falkirk Wheel

We were then joined by John & Penny, also by Fiona who is puppy walker coordinator and she came with a German Shepherd – very playful!

J & P took us to see the Kelpies – huge horse heads – impressive size and shapes:

The Kelpies

Now at John & Penny's home. Lovely to clean up, wash, have a meal and chat with them sitting on comfy chairs. Barney liking lying on carpets!

Day 98. 2/7 The Falkirk Wheel to Milton of Campsie

With John & Penny for another night	16 miles
Warm day again	649 ft

We were dropped off by John & Penny, carried light day sacks, so another 'easy' day.
After the 1000 mile point was reached we celebrated with a baked Camembert lunch followed by ice cream at the Boathouse near Kilsyth. Then it was on to meet Julie from Guide Dogs who walked with us at Kirkintilloch.
Penny then picked us up again and we were taken back to Menstrie for another night with her and John – a Big Thank You!

Penny & John dropped us back at Falkirk Wheel and we enjoyed the walk along the Forth & Clyde Canal – wider, more open, cleaner water, fresher air. Barney had a spring in his step and so did we, so we went quite fast.

A peaceful Forth & Clyde Canal

Highlights: sedge warblers, a buzzard calling and reaching the 1000 mile mark of the walk just before a marina with a cafe at Auchinstarry.

1000 miles reached

We celebrated with tea and a tapas type meal – whole warm Camembert with bread and salad. A change from the usual cheese sarnie!

Off again towards Kirkintilloch and met up with Julie from Glasgow Guide Dogs:

When we got to Milton of Campsie, Penny picked us up to drive us back over the Campsie Hills – another meal made for us, then lots of organising to do. A warm day.

Day 99. 3/7 Milton of Campsie to Drymen

Drymen Camping, Easter Drumquhassie	15 miles
Another hot day	811 ft

We were dropped off again by John and Penny and were able to walk lightly loaded as they delivered our bags to the Drymen campsite. They really have helped us along over the last few days, putting us up, ferrying us back and forth and getting things we need. Many thanks to you both.

The route taken is along a disused railway line, now a cycle track which unfortunately was tarmac and the day got hotter as we progressed. This resulted in blisters, the same as the last time we had these conditions in Devon. We did get our first view of mountains however – whoopee!

Penny and John kindly took our heavy packs onto Drymen campsite after dropping us back to Milton of Campsie where Penny picked us up yesterday. They have done a lot to help us, we've so enjoyed their house comforts and company, also had 3 bag free days too. We'll all get a shock tomorrow.

Today was very hot and walking on tarmac cycle paths, BLISTERS AGAIN! Even though with Compeed on, Bob's enlarged. I don't know how Lejog people do roads, just no give on your feet.

We followed an old rail line / cycle track to Strathblane, at least it was woody and shady, until the end where the sun was blasting down on the long track. We made it to a hotel garden for cold orange and a rest. Then picked up the track again, missing Strathblane and this time it was soft and muddy through trees – much better. It was past 2 before we emerged to meet the West Highland Way (and hard track again), needed to sit and eat yesterdays cheese sandwich (yesterday we 'dined' on Camembert with bruschetta at the marina).

No viewing spot to draw, so off again down a long, straight, hard, hot path which after 1 ½ miles had a pub at the end. Oh the bliss of a cup of tea for me, an orange for Bob, with our socks off and feet up in the shade on a bench. 5 miles still to go and 3 or 4pm by now, my blister sore too.

Hills in the distance – things to come...

We went quite well after the break, but Barney feeling the end of the day heat. Crossed a few roads and followed WHW signs, passing a hamlet with ice creams / drinks and an honesty box. Fantastic! Some Belgian boys said they wouldn't do that in Belgium. Onwards on the tarmac lane, uphill to finish of course and here we are in the small camp field, fortunately a breeze blowing with the sun out, so doors all open (so far) and feet horizontal!

Quiet a hard day with heat even though no weight to carry.

Day 100. 4/7 Drymen to Aberfoyle

Cobleland Campsite	9.8 miles
Very wet, thunder	1028 ft

The route was to be on the Rob Roy Way, but we ended up simply walking the minor road direct from Drymen to the campsite as it was raining and in cloud on the high parts. Not ideal with blisters but we survived and got into the site soon after 2 so an afternoon off for once.

The site is excellent (couldn't say that about yesterday's site) and the staff were very interested in our trip and Barney. We even got a very welcome cup of tea – much appreciated after 10 miles of road walking in the rain.

In tent at campsite by R. Forth whooshing along. Heavy rain and thunder in morning – we walked the road from Drymen in torrents!

I did a small shop in the Spar and went back to another shop to buy some American, very lightweight, plastic sandals for camp.

Long straight road

We decided to walk the tarmac in spite of blisters as it was a very quiet single track lane and we didn't fancy the longer route through forest. My heel blister is very sore.

Very friendly site staff when we arrived, they made us tea, said have pitch for free and made a big fuss of Barney. Here we are, in early for once, raining with sounds of the rushing river and other campers.

Barney's (and our) Pitch

Day 101. 5/7 Rest Day

We decided to stay another night and have a rest day at the Cobleland Campsite as it is such a lovely site. Excellent situation and facilities and Barney had his own pitch next to the River!
Thanks to Lesley and staff for a relaxing stay.

Day off, relax, read, recuperate, ring family

Card 13	Cobeland campsite S. of Aberfoyle
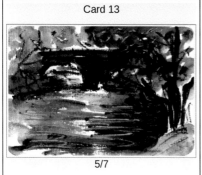 5/7	Dear Jane, sitting at door of tent by the R. Forth here. V. peaceful, Sunday. We are having a day off & it's v. nice to get up late, stay put, & relax!! Yesterday was a wet road slog from Drymen. The day before, a hot sun, tarmac cycle path – blister!! from the canal to Drymen. People on the blog think we are nearly there, but still long way up Scotland & lots of wild camps ahead. Looking forward to our route to Killin, Rannoch, FW etc – so good to read that Sal's mum going over for a month to help out, so we should finish the trip! Then what! Uh oh, clouds coming, looks like rain! - oh well, it's Scotland! Must be wonderful to have another grandbaby! Enjoy! Lots & lots of love from tent! Thinking of you Jos & B & B – woof! xx

Day 102. 6/7 Aberfoyle to Glen Finglas

Wild camp by Glen Finglas Reservoir	13.8 miles
Cleared to sunny and warm, then light rain later	2363 ft

> *Today we crossed the Highland Boundary Fault and into mountain country. First it was forest to Brig o' Turk and then we found a good wild camping spot next to the reservoir in Glen Finglas. Our first Glen of the trip.*

Left our very nice site, 5 star friendliness, scenery and facilities. We walked the river path to Aberfoyle. At a tea / sweet shop, we had coffee outside. I went back in to buy my drugs (treacle toffee). The lady serving came out and told us her husband was blind from the age of 2. Said how acutely he heard - "Use yer Lugs" he used to say!

Loch Drunkie

Uphill from Aberfoyle and into forest to follow a cycle track with hardish surface, zigzagging uphill. It got sunny and hot just where logging had cleared trees, so it was all open to the sun. After a break we joined a forest drive and met cars – grrr... Quite a hard packed surface now and heel sore, the track led down to a Loch Drunkie and a car park!

We saw a Guide Dog puppy walking car sticker and chatted to a woman who had been a puppy walker. She now has one of the 'failures' a labradoodle. That was 2 'blind' coincidences of the day, the 3rd was when we finally dropped down to Brig o' Turk and found an old byre, now a pub (cup of tea – wonderful) and the young girl behind the bar said she had a retriever / lab ex guide dog. So all 3 had cards given.

Glen Finglas

We took the path / road up Glen Finglas with the reservoir on our left. The road wound up steeply through mixed woodland, until opening out with loch and hill views. We are finally getting into the Highlands and it's beginning to look like it. The road turned to a rough track. We passed a sleepy bull, mums and calves, then kept on walking until the turn off we take tomorrow for Glen Meann.

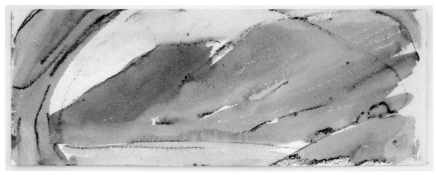
From tent in Glen Finglas

Now perched above the reservoir, water thundering down close by, with the shore and dark water out the tent 'window'. A bit of rain and wind, all cosy and full up after tea. Big flock of Canada geese on the water below, wonder what else we'll see?

Day 103. 7/7 Glen Finglas to Balquhidder

Balquhidder Braes Holiday Park, Balquhidder Station	12.3 miles
Wet start, then dried and warmed up later	1627 ft

The rain, forecast for last night, lasted all morning while we made our way over the hills to Balquhidder.

A wet start from our wild camp, but eased to light rain as we followed the track up Glenn Meann, negotiating a cow herd!

Lost the track, but found it at the bealach (pass), after that easy, soft going downhill all the way. Later we reached a farm track, then it was tarmac to Balquhidder. No painting today with all the rain. A quick sarnie on the bridge, with rain coming in over the loch in the west, and more road walking for a few miles to reach the main road.

A new friend

We went in a pub which used to be the Kingshouse. Very nice, and had gi-normous coffee cake with our juice. Hot now as we followed a cycle track to this campsite, located on a narrow strip of land right next to the main A84 road, and the loos are miles from our tent. It's really a static caravan site, cheap and cheerful. We had an evening meal at a restaurant across the road where the waitress told us that her mum breeds flatcoats and they had 4! We ate too much or our stomachs have shrunk!

Safety

Safety on a long trip takes some careful thought and planning before you start.

A range of issues have to be considered. Fortunately our previous experience of remote backpacking was beneficial.

Water. Fresh, clean water is not always readily available when backpacking. Campsites normally have a reliable, drinkable source but when wild camping it is often a case of using whatever is available nearby. Water can be carried but it greatly adds to an already heavy burden so in practice, a source close to where we camp is normally used. If the water was clear, then for cooking, it was boiled before use. If the source was contaminated or if it was to be used for drinking then it was filtered. For this, a water filter was used as shown in the picture:

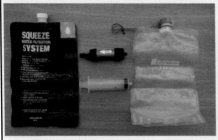

This consists of a 'dirty' 2 litre container in which the water is collected, filter to actually clean the water, 'clean' container into which the water is filtered and syringe used to clear the filter when it becomes blocked.

Two sets were carried which gave us 4 litres of water which was enough for the evening and following morning meals.

Cooking. Gas was our cooking fuel. This has two safety issues, Fire risk and carbon monoxide. To avoid problems we always cook in a porch with the door open. Our gas stove was pegged to the ground in a position to ensure no tent material (or other) could be ignited.

Illness and **Injury**. Minor illness and injuries would normally be dealt with from our basic first aid kits which we carried. More of a problem was when further assistance would be required.

For much of the trip this would be no different to being on a walk in the countryside where local help could be called on or at worst, a call-out to the emergency services using a mobile phone. In the remote parts of the Highlands however, we could be several hours walk from the nearest person and no mobile phone coverage. To cater for these conditions Bob carried a personal locator beacon (PLB). Activating the PLB would initiate a response from the search and rescue facilities within minutes – something only to be used in a serious emergency when it could be a life saver.

Day 104. 8/7 Balquhidder to Glen Lochay

Wild Camp on Glen hillside	14.5 miles
Sunny at times, cool breeze later on	1897 ft

A cycle track walk to Killin where we had tea and scones next to the falls. Then onto the shops to stock up for the next 4 days. Finally away from tarmac, and wild camping on an old path above Glen Lochay.
We can now see the mountains which made up the last round of Munros we did in 2012.
It's amazing how much snow is still about this far south in July.

We set off on a cycle track through woodland with views down to Lochearnhead. Did a painting of the loch:

Loch Earn

We zigzagged up to join the old railway line, now a new cycle path, surface ok, gravel mostly. We were above the A85 traffic in Glen Ogle.

Over a viaduct and at the head of the valley, we crossed the main road, the track left the old line (which used to go to Crianlarich) then walked a cycle path through woodland. Before though, a great view of the Tarmachan ridge we'd once climbed.

Feet had enough of cycle tracks and very glad to drop into Killin for tea and scones outside the Falls of Dochart Hotel.

Falls of Dochart

Spent a while in Killin, buying packet meals from the Outdoor shop, then in the Co-Op, followed by the dividing up, dog food and rations, on the bench outside. Sunny on the road walk (of course) as we plodded along out of town.

The Tarmachan Ridge and Ben Lawers

At a bridge, a van passed slowly and a woman driving waved. Just as we turned off onto the minor road up Glen Lochay, she stopped to ask "Are you the people walking Lejog?". She had seen an article about us in the MBA (Mountain Bothies Association) magazine and recognised the dog with his panniers! She was so pleased to have met us. Her name was Morvern and had done 12 TGO challenges[*] and lived in the South Cairngorms. What a chance meeting.

We had 2 or 3 miles plod in the late 'heat' on the road, wondering whether to camp by the river or head uphill. We passed a scout encampment on flat land, and nearly missed our intended track up the hillside – we took it, wondering why it was tarmac.

The zigzags in Glen Lochay

It led uphill in a series of zigzags to a wire fenced off wooded area, that said 'Danger of Drowning'?[†] We circumnavigated it all and picked up the old way – a track following the 300m contour or so round the hill.

* TGO Challenge is a major backpacking event crossing Scotland from east to west.
† We later found out that it is the surge shaft for Lochay Power Station which we passed earlier

Feels like an adventure now, off track and on new ground

Great views of Munros we've climbed, Ben Challum, Heasgarnich, Ben Ghaordaidh all laid out before us. Even patches of SNOW on them! We found a flat pitch eventually, a bit exposed, but no midges in this breeze, brrrr – chilly too. Now to paint the view, after a good meal called **Adventure Food!**

Ben Challum

Day 105. 9/7 Glen Lochay to Cam Chreag

Wild camp beyond Bridge of Balgie	12.6 miles
Sun on and off	2618 ft

Another wild camp at nearly 2000ft well beyond Bridge of Balgie. We were fortunate to meet somebody who could suggest the best way across to Rannoch so we changed our route.

A long hard day today; started sunny as we packed up to follow the old way, contouring around the hillside with old sleepers crossing bogs and iron rail tracks making balancing bridges.

A while since the last broken bridge

Need to look at the history of this area, the path led to shielings, ruins of small buildings, just stone rectangles left. When were they abandoned? The Clearances I expect.

Once we reached the high ground, we saw we had a long pathless boggy way to go to reach the top of the bealach. We found a quad bike track winding its way round peat hags, but we lost it after a while and made our own way through the bogs.

It was similar to Kinder or Killhope, but miles of it. We thought once we reached the bealach, the descent would be obvious, but again we lost any sign of an 'old way' and took a tiring route through heather on deer / sheep tracks.

Peat hags

We'd come down the Lairig Breisleich (with difficulty) 5hrs for 6 miles. Both glad to reach the small, single track road running downhill to Bridge of Balgie in Glen Lyon, tired though, tarmac hard on tired feet. So glad to find tea rooms / shop / PO not too far off the junction. Sat and drank pot of tea, bought tuna sarnies, cake and finished with a Magnum. Chatted to a shepherd about the route to take, and set off in hot sun, along the Glen Lyon road until the turn off. Now we were on a sandy track following a stream, the Allt a Choire Uidhre, up and up it went. I 'got through' all the hornpipes I could remember.[*]

Another end of day long ascent

[*] I play the B/C Button Accordion, I couldn't add that to my load! I find concentrating on humming sets of tunes in my head, helps the miles pass when the going gets tough.

238

After 6k we finally stopped, once over the bealach. We'd been following the boggy track of an Argocat* until we found running water and luckily flat ground nearby. So here we are footsore and weary, tea cooked and eaten. 9:15pm writing and reading. Outside, the burble of a stream running and a light breeze. We are miles from anyone. Feels adventurous, but normal for us too! Great to be on new terrain, yet linking up with mountains we've climbed – An Stuc and Ben Lawers behind us as we walked. Cam Chreag, a Corbett is 1000ft above us and ½ mile away, but think we'll give it a miss – Another day. Tomorrow we walk to Rannoch Moor.

Birds – pippets, wheatear, and heard 2 times, a disturbed raptor – sounded peregrine like – both in the valleys we walked today.

Day 106. 10/7 Cam Chreag to near Rannoch Station

Wild camp by the Allt Eigheach	11.8 miles
Light rain, muggy but breeze later	1073 ft

The shepherds advice yesterday, for the route, helped us reach Loch Rannoch more easily. We then walked toward Rannoch Station and took the track north to Ossian. Unfortunately it is now a building site as small hydro schemes are being installed and the path is now a road. We found a good camping spot however and enjoyed the remote location and extensive views.

Packed and away in rain by 8am – it was only light though and clouds stayed on the mountain tops. We followed the old track, looking out for the posts stuck in strategic places as it led us towards the bealach we wanted to go up.

As I walked, I imagined leading a Highland Pony up the track, it was brown with a black mane. I felt its presence at my shoulder as I held its rope halter…

* Argocat – All terrain vehicle used by estate and game keepers

Not much of a track

Near the top of the bealach, Bob lost confidence in the old way as it seemed to be heading uphill – it was, taking a more direct route over the shoulder of the hill, avoiding bogs and steep gullies. We found our own way, across the heather, with the Allt Leac Ghiubhais below us.

No paths here

It took just 2 hours from camp to the junction where after 'crossing' a deer fence by a high stile (Barney going under), we met a track. Now we followed another old way. Lovely when we can still see and use them, and not made up by estates with hard compacted gravel. This one was very boggy and contoured around a small hill until we joined a more solid track leading down to the hamlet, Bridge of Gaur. We came out onto a road at a padlocked gate with an estate sign on the other side 'WARNING DEER SHOOTING 1st July etc. etc.' - grrrrr bloody estates – think they own the place!

We climbed over and got Barney under, then a long tarmac road walk began, muggy, midgy and very quiet as it led to a 'dead end', Rannoch Station. Most cars actually slowed down to pass. After 4 miles or so, we turned off for a footpath to Fort William, going over Rannoch Moor, but OH No, it had been turned into a hard gravel track due to some hydro works going on – grrrrr...

Rannoch Moor path, now a vehicle track, grrr

We plodded on, the mountain views getting more and more exciting. The Bridge of Orchy hills appeared from behind cloud, looking dramatic, as we watched the little train pull out from Rannoch Station:

Train leaving Rannoch Station

Mind we were both tired and tetchy, ready to stop, luckily a breeze and no midges. We found a lovely, grassy spot to pitch the tent by the river Allt Eigheach.

Wild camping on Rannoch Moor

Revived after a cup of tea, now relaxed, I went outside in late sunshine to paint hills and clouds. Meal over, reading our Kindles in the tent, bit of rain now, river rushing along in a hurry.

PS Saw whinchat or stone chat? Black head, white stripes chestnut brown breast.

Card 14	Camped by Allt Eigheach near track from rd to Rannoch Stn → Corour. Fortunately a breeze is up otherwise it would be midgy hell!! We've had long days of rough walking on very 'old ways' yesterday up to sheilings from Glen Lochay to Glen Lyon by a remote glen & Bealach then camped under a Corbett with snow patches on! & this morning just picked out an old track up & over into another glen before dropping down to Loch Rannoch & on to here, where the track is modern & nasty hoggin – due to dam building or something. We stopped at 4pm for a change, so I had time to paint! 8 I think – here's yours! V. dark moody skies. Lots love ol gypsy Jos xxxx
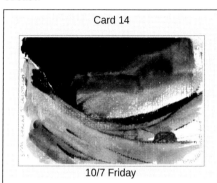 10/7 Friday	

Day 107. 11/7 Allt Eigheach to the Abhainn Rath (Staoineag)

Wild camp opposite Staoineag Bothy next to the Abhainn Rath	13.8 miles
Grey day with drizzle, rain to end the day	1367 ft

One wild camp to another. Today we went via Loch Ossian and Corrour Station which we know well from previous trips – wonderful country!

Writing to sound of rain pattering on the tent and roar of waterfalls which I can see through my end 'window'. Pitched just after 4pm again which is good – time to relax, brew tea and eat oatcakes, and paint.

This morning, we had an 8 mile walk along the track to Corrour Station where we assumed the cafe was still there for coffee. The hard compacted track, put in for major hydro-electric construction work, fortunately gave way to sand for most of the way.

It was grey, but wonderful panoramas across the moor to the mountains west – the Black Mount, Glen Etive, the Buchaille and the distant Black-water reservoir. I would've stopped to paint, but light drizzle on and off so it's in my memory bank!

Loch Ossian with youth hostel in trees

We dropped down to familiar ground, the track by Loch Ossian passing the YHA at the end of the loch and on to the station – no cafe, grrrrr, (now an evening restaurant). Oh well, we rested on the platform seat, found we had phone signal, so I rang Joanna who sounded chirpy. Then a new way for us, on an old track on the west side of the railway line till we arrived at the south shore of Loch Treig. Nearby Munro tops were all in cloud, the views up the loch dramatic, with dark clouds at the northern end – I painted.

Loch Treig looking west up Easan Dubh

Lunch break attention

Next, an enjoyable boggy path! Round the head of the loch, all quiet, offshore islands in still water, saw 2 mergansers and heard the peep of sandpipers.

Pitched next to Abhainn Rath

Once over the river bridge by an old lodge, Creaguaineach, we turned left for the footpath to Fort William and made our way along till we found this lovely pitch by the rushing river.

Day 108. 12/7 Abhainn Rath to Fort William

Glen Nevis Campsite, Fort William	14.7 miles
Rain, drying up as the day went on.	1412 ft

A wet day along the Glen Nevis path which was very boggy with the steady rain. A stop at Steall and then the road and forest track to Glen Nevis campsite.
We met somebody searching for his friend who went missing 10 days ago, and then the RAF Mountain Rescue team looking for the same person as well as another man missing since May – all rather sad but it reminds us how this can be a very unforgiving place.

Here we are back in civilization, buying food and WINE from the site shop and getting caught up on phones. I rang brother Steve and surprised him. Jo sounds happy with her new bike.

Heading for Glen Nevis next to the swollen river

We had a rough, wet walk from our spot by the falls, which with overnight rain, had changed to all thundering foaming water. Maybe the sound kept me awake as I didn't sleep well. We met a party of girls from Sheffield doing their Gold Duke of Edinburgh award.

After a mile or so we came across an MBA bothy at Meananach, very well done up and supplied.

Meannanach Bothy

Would've been good to stop, but we plodded on, it was hard work, continually watching feet for bogs, as well as plodging across 'fords'. Soon stopped bothering avoiding water and went straight through it. Pity it rained, as it stopped us sitting and taking in the mountains but they were in cloud. Did however see the Mamores, Binnein Beag and Binnein Mor, as well as the bealach where we once camped on the Grey Corries. Quite something to remember all our adventures climbing up the Munros especially our backpacking hike with Barney across from Cairngorm to Ben Nevis over all the 4000 ft peaks.

Nearing Glen Nevis

We met a lone figure, a man, who asked if by chance we were from Mountain Rescue, he'd seen the dog panniers. He said the team were out searching for a friend of his who had gone missing, also another man, both since May. Probably Munro climbers, like ourselves – how sad. The helicopter flew up and down the glen. Eventually we began meeting people, families out for a walk to see the Steall Falls.

We stopped for our lunch break opposite the falls, before leaving by the gorge path.

Steall Falls

When we met the glen road end, we began the long walk to the campsite, finding a forest track, with views down to the road. It was quite a plod until, at last, a track downhill taking us straight to the Glen Nevis Restaurant, where they DON'T take dogs inside. Grrrrr... We had a pint outside, before walking to the campsite, booking in and shopping in their well equipped shop.

Pasta for tea and tinned fruit! Bob is getting carried away blogging (see page 252). Nice to feel clean after showers. Meeting friends, Geoff, Wendy and dog Meg in Fort William tomorrow.

Food

As we were backpacking, our route often meant overnight stays without the luxury of pubs and restaurants close by. Also, having a dog often ruled out entry to food establishments. Because we didn't know exactly where we would be staying each night we therefore ensure we always carried enough food regardless of situation. This was particularly important in the Scottish Highlands where we were often days without shops. Meal planning and distribution of food were important tasks prior to the start of the trip. Fortunately we had plenty of previous experience of what was needed for our rations.

Cooking equipment is minimal and lightweight – a tiny gas stove, gas canister, wind-shield and 2 pans, 2 of each plastic mugs, bowls and spoons cover all culinary requirements. Barney has a fold up bowl but mostly ate off the ground.

Breakfast was either muesli or porridge to take us through the morning, along with several tea brews. Late morning included snacking on fruit and nut mix (scroggin).

Soon after midday, we'd eat a sandwich prepared by Jos earlier while Bob was making the porridge. An afternoon snack of an energy bar, along with fruit and nut mixes during the day, kept us going to camp time.

Occasionally we had other sources of goodies found en route (oh those Cornish cream teas and pasties) – not common in the Highlands of Scotland alas.

Our regular evening meals were a highlight of the day – time to relax and recover from the days exertions. The meal normally included 3 courses – soup, main and pudding. Soup was routinely Cup–A–Soup packet with boiled water, main course, a dehydrated meal with added boiled water, and pudding – cake with an instant custard made with, you guessed it, boiled water. All in all, along with cups of tea, a fulfilling meal with which we rehydrated – an important task after a days walk. The meal required lots of water which we always found locally, sometimes coloured brown from peaty streams as can be seen in the image above (no, it's not what you think it is!).

Day 109. 13/7 Rest Day

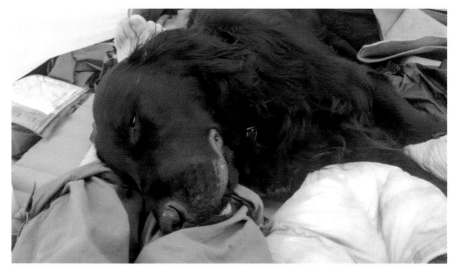

Sleepy dog

A lie in! Rain in the morning so washing and drying of clothes using campsite laundry facilities. Then walked into Fort William to meet G & W[*] and went to a dog friendly pub for lunch and a good chat. We shopped for our next stage and they gave us a lift back to the campsite. A sunny evening but dramatic cloud on the Ben[†], I did paintings.

Clouds on the Ben

[*] Geoff & Wendy live in Arisaig. Jos became friends with Wendy on the Isle of Muck – Jos on painting trips and Wendy teaching at the school. They discovered a shared passion, walking and dogs.
[†] Ben Nevis, highest mountain in Britain at 1345m (4411ft), commonly just called 'The Ben'

The Route of the last few days

I thought I'd set the records straight with some notes on where we've been recently.

The Andy Robinson End to End Trail Guide we are following uses the West Highland Way to get from Drymen to Fort William. We have already done that so we devised a more remote alternative.

Our route took us to Aberfoyle and then through the forest to Brig o' Turk where we went over a pass to Balquhidder. The Callander to Oban railway line route, now a cycle track followed and we branched off to Killin. Over a non extant 'drove road' to Bridge of Balgie and then what turned out to be an old route not marked on O.S. maps to Rannoch. The route then took the Rannoch Moor track through to Corrour Station and then on to Glen Nevis – The Wet 'n Wild Way!

Nearly there?

Some Facebook comments suggest we've nearly finished – it doesn't feel like that.

Here are some facts about what's to come…

• 243 miles.

• From Fort William to Watten and the trail passes one small village with shops, four isolated hotels, a bunkhouse and a youth hostel – that's it! Only 12 public roads are crossed in over 200 miles of walking.

• We will be going off trail to stop in Ullapool for a rest day and resupplies. We are having other resupplies posted to two Inns to be picked up en route (thanks Lucy).

• We may have to change the route if the weather is not favourable as we have to cross some rivers which are impassable after heavy rain.

We've still a challenge ahead.

Section 6. The Northern Highlands and the Flow Country

Fort William to John o' Groats

14 nights wild camp, 1 bothy, 1 pub and 7 campsites	259.2 miles
Most days wet at times but with some sunny intervals, cool. Sun to finish	31508 ft

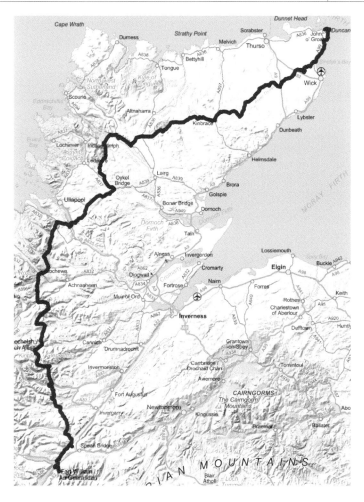

This last stage of our walk took us into wild, isolated, uninhabited land, often challenging pathless terrain. Perfect! It did rain a lot, but that kept the Scottish midges away, mostly. I did paint wearing a midgy net some evenings outside the tent. Those paintings have midges stuck to them! Leaving a sunny Fort William by the ease of the Caledonian canal tow path, our route took us up over many high mountain passes, and back down into remote glens, Glen Garry, Glen Shiel, Glen Affric, Glen Elchaig until we could resupply at the village shop of Kinlochewe.

Craig á Mhaim, South Shiel Ridge

We waded streams turned to torrents after heavy rain, we saw dramatic sunsets over lochs as skies cleared. We watched a red throated diver giving out its eerie call on a grey, light flickered pool, reflecting cloud, sky and rock. We passed the hefty shapes of the Torridon mountains we'd climbed, Liathach, Ben Eighe.

Entering the remote country north of Kinlochewe

More remote land after Kinlochewe, stopping to paint and 'take in' Slioch, the Fisherfield mountains, and mighty An Teallach brooding in clouds, camping by the shores of remote Loch an Nid.

Reaching a busy main road, a sunny Ullapool was a shock to the system. We enjoyed a weekend, relaxing? Well, plenty of washing and re supplying to do before the next long stage.

Back to civilization briefly – Ullapool Ferry terminal

Now our route left the west coast, and led north east, crossing the watershed over a pass as we headed for the river Oykel. Another rushing, swollen river to camp by, then skirting round the great massif of Ben More Assynt, camping on a boggy bealach to reach the head of Loch Shin and on to the remote Crask Inn.

River Oykel

The high mountains were left behind as we made for the coast over the notoriously boggy flow country. The Knockfin Heights, our last hills were very hard going, with endless peat hags to jump across! A relief to reach flatter going alongside the river Thurso where we watched an osprey fishing.

Nearing camp, Morven in the distance

Later, we crossed the busy A9 road, plunging into forest, and back to farm tracks and minor roads, until before us lay the sea at Sinclair's Bay on the east coast. One more day to go, in sunshine, a blue sky, sea breezy day along the coastal field edges with stunning cliffs and stacks up to Duncansby Head.

Duncansby Head and Orkney in the distance

The land ended, we could walk north no longer. The Orkney Islands on the horizon. We reluctantly turned the corner and there was John o' Groats – the end of our walking.

Day 110. 14/7 Fort William to GairLochy

Gairlochy Holiday Park	12.4 miles
Sunny start and dry day	580 ft

Met up with friends Geoff & Wendy who helped us out yesterday. Today, Geoff took our bags and Wendy, along with their dog Meg, walked with us. Barney had a playmate.

After making our way out of Fort William (and seeing the steam engine – The Hogwarts Express bound for Mallaig) we reached the Caledonian Canal which we followed to Gairlochy along the towpath. Not normal walking for Wendy who is more used to climbing the mountains around here. Plenty of activity on the canal however, including meeting an Australian who is cycling around Britain in 80 days! Ben Nevis appeared out of the cloud just for us.

The Ben was clear to start. Geoff & Wendy met us at 8:30am and we drove to Fort William, where we began today's walk from the Lidl car park! (we walked this stretch yesterday)

Following Andy R's route from the town, by the river, then railway (saw steam train), we ended up at Neptune's Staircase at Corpach. The canal route was easy, especially with no packs, as Geoff had them in their campervan. Barney bombed along.

Discussing the route

We caught up a lone woman backpacker, Noana from Vienna. She'd just done the West Highland Way and now on the Cape Wrath Trail, taking the low level route. Her sack was very heavy – a monster!

Caledonian Canal and Noana with her monster rucksack

We had a good chat, tempted to ask her to join us, but she would've been dependent on us re. route, so we didn't. Might meet up again, who knows. She draws and paints too. We also had an Australian cyclist touring the British Isles at our lunch table by the canal.

Geoff met us at Gairlochy and we were treated to tea in their camper. He dropped us off at the Gairlochy campsite we've camped at before. Very peaceful at the moment, no-one around. In sunshine here, but dark clouds on the Ben – I painted. Feel tired, perhaps the cycle path?

Day 111. 15/7 Gairlochy to River Garry

Wild camp at end of Loch Poulary	15.9 miles
Sunny day, hot work at times	2865 ft

A varied day. First lochs Lochy and Arkaig, then a pass over to Glen Garry.

This morning, Bob picked up Archie's Story pictures and message re. his recent op, to try to remove the tumour. One showed him just before 'going under' and one after. A shock for us, seeing his bald head – poor wee man, but the good news is that they left his nose on! Goodness knows how they did the surgery. Now a wait till Friday for results, hoping cancer all gone. Poor Sal & Dan, what a time they are having. We sent messages and got a reply from Dan, so that was good before we're out of range.

We had a lovely sunny day for a change. Walked down the road, passing a woman in her garden, who commented 'What's that big round yellow thing in the sky?' She had a malamute (a husky like dog) which howled as we went by!

We joined the canal where we 'left off' yesterday, crossed it and walked for a while in a forest, then down to the side of Loch Lochy. A very pleasant start, in the shade of trees at the lochside, a peaceful expanse of water. We looked back at views of the Ben with Carn Mor Dearg, all crisp and dark, the Ben showing its craggy, steep N face with snow in the gullies.

The north faces of Carn Mor Dearg and Ben Nevis still holding snow in July

It was hot walking and we stopped for some fun at the loch. Barney cooled off enjoying a swim.

A rare sight – Barney having a swim

Not so rare sight – grandma playing

Next, up to the road again and soon off onto tracks to Achnacarry, in estate woodland, passing an old church until we reached a bridge at the end of Loch Arkaig. We had a bit of road walking, very quiet for traffic and then we got a surprise at the junction where our route was to follow a burn up to a bealach (Allt Dubh). The hydro works were there as at the Rannoch track – yellow diggers, pipes, bags of concrete, men in white hats...

Another path turned into a micro hydro-electric scheme track

The track was sandy and made up a long way, so we plodded up in the heat, with wonderful views opening up as we gained height.

We looked back to the Ben, the Aonachs and the Grey Corries and west down Loch Arkaig to the Munros we'd climbed. It took a big effort to keep going and climb up to the bealach. Once the track petered out, we had rough

ground as we followed the stream, on and on, up and up, aiming for the lowest point on the skyline.

View back to Ben Nevis

Our efforts were rewarded, as once on the top of the bealach, a panorama of peaks opened up from west to east and beyond to the north, Beinn Sgritheall, all the Forcan Ridge, Kintail and Glen Affric hills:

To think we've climbed all the highest ones in the area, it never ceases to amaze. What memories of expeditions we've had up here and all over Scotland, most with Barney.

We reluctantly peeled away from such sights and made our way over pathless terrain, downhill following a stream.

Heading north to Glen Garry and beyond

We did follow an old track contouring round a hill eventually, very unused and boggy. We kept going as Bob was worried about a river crossing. In the end he needn't have been. Since the guide book was published, a big tract of forestry has been felled and new hard roads put in AND a new bridge! It was tiring walking on the hard track, and again what was once a grassy 'cart track', now a man made surface and industrialised with forestry trucks, diggers, safety notices, not 'wild Scotland' anymore. We found a flat, grassy spot, by little Loch Poulary as soon as we crossed the bridge over the very fast flowing, roaring, River Garry. It was wide and looked beautiful in the evening sun. The usual recovering, and then food to cook, so by the time that was over, the midges were out. Time for bed.

Day 112. 16/7 River Garry to Cluanie Inn

Wild camp next to old road bridge, Cluanie Inn	10.7 miles
Warm and sunny to start, gradually changing	2223 ft

Reached the pub and our resupply box. May stay a day which would put our schedule back.

When we left this morning Barney started limping badly – especially so on the tarmac, much easier on the grass. I gave him a double dose of Loxicom, the medication I'd been carrying 'just in case'. Once we turned off onto the rough, peat heather track he was fine, leading the way but very ready for a rest.

We had an uphill to a bealach first, warm going as another fine day. From the top, a great view to the South Shiel Ridge and peaks beyond, and below, a remote Glen Loyne with its meandering river.

Another bealach and time to take in the views

Once Bob managed to open 2 deer fence gates (wire and knotted rope) we got down to the flats, crossed the river and had our lunch. I sketched looking upstream, Munros we'd 'done' earlier when camped at Kinloch Hourn way down the end of the glen.

Then time for more up, this time we followed an ATV track weaving its way up steeply, in contrast to the gentle pony route earlier. Now we joined the old road to Skye – tarmac again. Barney started limping so I kept him to the grass. It seemed a long way down.

The old Skye road

We were caught up and accompanied by a couple 'out for the day' - first people in 2 days.

We finally reached the Inn and collected our supplies parcel, I had a whole pot of tea, Bob a beer and later returned to pitch by the river as NO ROOM at the INN!

We went back for an evening drink and a meal, I had haggis, neeps and tatties! We both had cranachan for pud, followed by a Talisker. Very nice – very filling too. Chatted to 2 men, one knew Nikki from Guide Dogs as his wife is a puppy walker. Small world.

Looking west into Glen Shiel

Now back in the tent, river burbling, tent flapping, heavy rain and gales forecast. Decided to stop tomorrow to give Barney a rest. Hope he recovers to continue, not sure if it's a muscle or paw problem.

Day 113. 17/7 River Cluanie Rest Day because of Barney

Days 113 – 117 Cluanie Inn – Kinlochewe

A hard few days as we had 50mph winds at Cluanie and plenty of rain throughout. Fortunately the rain came at the right times and the rivers were low when we needed to cross them.

We have been walking through areas we know from climbing Munros but it's novel linking them all up together in a linear walk. Some parts have been easier than expected and some harder, but that's the way it goes...

Gales and rain, so noisy night last night.

Sobering morning and day as read and later talked to Dan re. Archie's results after his op. - disappointing as cancer still there, spreading out, so he needs chemo, and radiotherapy for the next few months.

Just been to pub, Barney still limping slightly on tarmac hmmm... Probably risk the walk tomorrow as it's all soft going.

The Cluanie Inn and our way north through the glen

Card 15	Friday again! But posted Kinlochewe. Loch Cluanie from tent. Veils of rain today, having had a day here to rest Barney, who had a limp on hard ground yest, but fine on soft. Hope he's OK for next 4 days as we head into 'wilderness' to Kinlochewe. Feeling grey myself today after speaking to Dan – v. upset over A's results after op. Praps you've seen it on FB by now. Cancer still there, so now radiotherapy & chemo. Hope to god it works. Makes everything else seem unimportant.
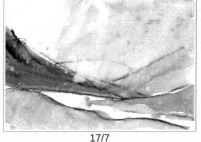 17/7	We'll keep going as long as we can. Would be good to finish now we are this far on. Still some tough walking – the best ahead! Got used to this tent life – cars, people – all seem too much!! getting reclusive!! Had a good day with Wendy, Geoff & Meg! They walked canal with us! Xx

Day 114. 18/7 Cluanie Inn to Glen Gaorsaic

| Wild camp above Loch a'Bhealaich | 11.1 miles |
| Very wet day, sun appears at very end | 1712 ft |

In the pub in the eve, we met Noana again, the Austrian woman, attempting the Cape Wrath Trail solo. She came back to pitch her tent next to ours. What a rough night, wind really buffeting the tent and heavy rain, such a loud roar of river. Didn't sleep for ages. Up at 6 as determined to start this remote stretch of walking. We packed up and walked together in the driving rain all morning, through a very boggy glen, An Caorann Mor leading over a bealach to Glen Affric. The streams were torrents, milky white cascading down the mountain sides and we just had to wade across some. Noana was so glad of our company, she'd not have managed alone. Bob helped us both over one or two rivers in spate.

It was just 3 ¼ hours from the main road to the red roofed YHA Alltbeithe, a welcome sight with smoke coming from the chimney, Yey! The friendly woman warden gave us fresh baked scones and coffee and tea.

I was soaked, socks, boots, top and trousers – Goretex? Thought it could stand heavy rain – hmmm... We had a good hour there, then took our leave after exchanging addresses as Noana was booked in for the night. We put wet things on again and headed west up Glen Gniomhaidh path leading to Bealach an Sgairne. Once we had previously descended from Ben Fhada to this bealach and ascended the Munro A' Ghlas-bheinn.

We turned off the main path to veer north, alongside Lochs a' Bhealaich and Gaorsaic. Now, pitched on a slope, above the loch, sound of water pouring down behind us. We think we are fine ie not in line of flood and phew, wind is dropping.

Loch a Bhealaich

A wet, hard day, I'm warming legs in sleeping bag. Damp things hanging up in tent. Really ready for the hot tea and soup.

Sun tried to shine briefly so after tea, I did a painting of the bealach at sunset.

Sunset behind Bealach an Sgàirne

A comfortable, no wind night.

Day 115. 19/7 Glen Gaorsaic to Maol-bhuide

Wild camp next to Maol Bhuide Bothy	11.5 miles
Rain and sun throughout the day	1877 ft

We decided on a change of route here. More rain overnight left us thinking it might be difficult to get Barney down the side of the Falls of Glomach. This is one of the most spectacular parts of the whole trail as the falls are amongst the best in Britain. It meant crossing pathless terrain for several miles and then picking up an old path down to Carnach*.

We stopped for a break before continuing to Iron Lodge and up and over the bealach to the bothy at Maol-bhuidhe. Jos was hoping to try out the top bedroom in the bothy which had been occupied the last time we were here but it was not to be, as a couple with a dog arrived 2 minutes before us.

Light rain this morning, wet tent and gear all on as we packed up, but sun came out and we were soon walking along with 'everything' hanging out to dry.

To start with, no path as we made our way on the boggy hillside above the loch, a 'quad' track guided us above peat hags on higher ground and we looked down on another pair of remote lochs, a heron guarding – like a sentry on one.

Gleann Gaorsaic

* We trekked this on the Cape Wrath Trail.

As we crossed over the high ground at a bealach I heard and watched a wader – alarm calling, couldn't be sure what it was. Later though on another quiet lochan, I saw a red throated diver on its own and it gave its eerie cry too. Very evocative of wild places. As we got nearer it moved to the other end of the loch. We had a long steep descent down to Carnach, a cottage in Glen Elchaig. Back on familiar territory now, looking back at Loch na Leitreach where we camped last June.

Glen Elchaig

Both felt weary on the long sometimes steep ascent at the head of the glen after Iron Lodge, following quite a stony cart track for Barney but no limp, phew.

Long plod to Maol-bhuidhe bothy

Grit teeth and plod to the top, then still a long plod down the muddy track till finally Maol-bhuidhe bothy in sight:

The very remote Maol-bhuidhe bothy

An isolated cottage with mountains, lochs and rivers for miles. Disappointingly, another couple with a terrier turned up and Bob got grumpy as they let it bounce round Barney. Doh, was looking forward to a night in the old place, but didn't fancy sharing it with the terrier, so here we are feet up in the tent, resting after a 3 course meal. Cluanie cakes, yum pudding. Better go and wash up – pan and 2 plates!

Walking

Put one foot in front of the other and off you go... Well, not quite. We had to decide on footwear, socks and what clothes to wear before we even started. Then, conditions changed and so did the boots and clothes. Both leather and canvas boots were worn.

Which boots? Bob's selection before we started

We started with lightweight boots, but both changed to more robust, slightly heavier mountain boots as they offered better cushioning around and below the foot. 2 pairs of socks, one thin inner along with a thicker outer mostly avoided blisters although we realised that this combination is perhaps not best when in hot conditions.

We found on previous backpacking trips that trekking poles were advantageous, mostly helping with stability over uneven ground and when the weather made for difficult walking conditions as in gales. They were particularly beneficial on long upward and downward slopes, helping to push up and balancing on the way down, saving the knees.*

We have mentioned blisters before and an ongoing task was ensuring we didn't suffer them. Most of the time, not a problem, but the first signs of trouble and Compeed patches were applied.

Barney had Mushers pad protection applied daily and this worked very well – he had less of a problem with walking than we did! Mushers softened his foot pads and ensured that salt and grit didn't impede progress. He also carried specially made 'dog boots' in case of pad damage but these were never needed.

* And essential when fording swollen rivers

Day 116. 20/7 Maol-bhuidhe to Pollan Buidhe

Wild camp next to the Allt a Chonais	12.2 miles
Grey but stayed dry until the end of the day	2486 ft

Again, we are travelling through country we know but by new routes. It's nice to feel that you know an area but still see things with a different perspective. This day took us over another high pass – the Bealach Bhearnais before dropping down to Pollan Buidhe. As with many days now we are in more remote country, the walking consists of a mix of land rover tracks, old paths and sections of pathless terrain.

The bridge at Pollan Buidhe is nothing more than a wire and a hand-line to hang on to. The water level was low however, so we just walked across.

Barney seemed to have his picture taken a few times today.

A grey, but dry start, too cool for midges.

Got across the main river from Loch Cruoshie without getting feet wet, then a slog up slopes to reach an old path at the foot of Ben Dronaig[*]. This led us over the peat to the head of Loch Calavie – saw another red throated diver. Our walk now on a good but stony track alongside the loch.

Loch Calavie

Looking back we could see the Mullardoch Munros with tops in cloud. Onwards up and over a bealach to nearly reach Bendronaig Lodge, a neat looking place in the middle of nowhere. We turned right, on a track above

---

* A Corbett that Barney and I did on our own in a fog.

273

Loch an Laoigh, then a 4WD vehicle came up and unloaded 7 people to go fishing. Weird to see.

We had the shoulder of Ben Tharsuinn to climb up to the Bealach Bhearnais – hard going as no path, but we slogged on:

Barney waits for mum.

Relief to get up and realise we'd been there before to climb the Munros including 'Cheesecake' (Bidein a Choire Sheasgaich) in drought / heat conditions.

We stopped so I could paint the glen and mountainsides leading to Strathconon, then down to the river crossing:

When we got down to where we thought we'd camp, a gusty strong wind funnelled down the glen, we tried the flysheet up, mended ANOTHER tear and decided to move lower. Fortunately not far, to a more sheltered grassy spot right by the river. I can hear waterfalls close by too – rain, waterfall, river and wind. Clouds are rising up the valley and also down. A night in, reading after tea.

Day 117. 21/7 Pollan Buidhe to Kinlochewe

Wild camp just before Kinlochewe	13.9 miles
Wet start, gradually drying to a fine end	2190 ft

Down, up, down day to get to the edge of Kinlochewe. Again, mixed walking with tracks and an awkward section before Kinlochewe. We're actually on the Cape Wrath trail until Inverlael near Ullapool and this section has been mentioned in a number of forum posts about how awkward it is. Previously we have avoided it.

We had another hard day, a good start though. Packed up and walked down a track in the wet (just enough to put hoods up) to reach the main road and TRAFFIC. Grrrr... 1K walk along it, not too bad. Achnashellach Estate welcomes walkers and manages the deer for habitat survival – ha! Right next to deer fence, on the estate side, bare, the other side, wooded and full of birdsong!

Glen Carron

We took a track off the road to the Coulin Pass, an old pony track. It was steep up through the trees and a puff.

We soon reached a forest track and the top of the pass – gradually the Munros we'd climbed from Achnashellach Station lost their cloud cover. It's good to look back on all our Munro expeditions and link the places up with these tracks. We went at a good pace downhill to reach Loch Coulin before rising up again through forest.

Torridon hills

A track led us over moorland, but hard going as very boggy and tiring. The worst was yet to come as we entered a cut down forest, then pathless, crossing streams, head high bracken, bog and more bog! Oh for the road! But we hate roads really! When we'd made it through and reached clearer ground, I suggested stopping and camping, leaving the shop and PO for tomorrow. So here we are pitched on a hillside and the sun came out but so did the midges. Wonderful views. I painted wearing my midge net.

Liathach from tent

Slioch from the wild camp

Beinn Eighe to one side and Slioch to the other. Suddenly we are in the land of the Torridon giants, rising up steep and bare, with red, grey hues to the rock. Liathach looked very high in cloud. Hard to believe we summited all of these Munros with Barney. Now a roar – river, falls, wind – rarely do we go to bed without the sound of water.

Thinking of Dan as we reconnect with Facebook and see Archie had big Op. and nose job – bless – What next?

Day 118. 22/7 Kinlochewe to Loch an Nid

Wild camp at head of Loch an Nid	11.3 miles
Dry, cool with some brightness to start	2125 ft

Taking a different route to Loch an Nid for us, via the Heights of Kinlochewe and Lochan Fada then heading into remote, pathless territory.
Loch an Nid is a wonderful place to camp with a superb view of An Teallach in the distance.

A bright start at our camp with mountain views of Beinn Eighe and Slioch. We were only 5 minutes from the village and made for the shop, FOOD!

I posted my sketchbook, same man as always, quiet, reserved, his wife friendly and from Barnard Castle. They made a fuss of Barney tied up outside. We bought enough supplies for 2 days, and treated ourselves to cappuccino, coffee and croissants chocolait! Very welcome outside on the picnic tables.

Setting off fully laden, this time we headed for a track up from Incheril to the Heights of Kinlochewe. It was good going above the Abhainn Bruachaig which feeds into the Kinlochewe River, the gradient was easy and we reached the bealach without tiring. When the harder surface ended, it was wet and boggy but ok all the way up to Lochan Fada.

Lochan Fada and the Fisherfield Munros

The scenery was breathtaking, a backcloth of peaks from Slioch to our left swinging round to the Fisherfield Munros and Mullach Coire Fhearchair. Still amazing to think we've backpacked to the top of them all with Barney. Through a gap, south where we'd come from, the Torridons stood out.

Rain showers swept in, but thin veils and not very wetting (for a change). At the loch we turned right and made our way up rough hillside aiming for

Bealach na Croise – we found a way, easier than last time and made it to the bealach again not feeling too pushed.

Approaching the Bealach na Croise

A Go Bar to renew energy, then a path all the way downhill to Loch an Nid.

We crossed the river and decided to pitch on a lovely flat spot next to it with a fantastic view of An Teallach from the tent door.

I've had a go at painting the range, dark brooding peaks with clouds 'smoking' off the pointy pinnacles, that's why it's called the Forge. Again, we've actually climbed it.

An Teallach from tent

It is very satisfying thinking 'been up there'. To think we've walked all this way, to say hello to these great mountains.

This morning, outside the shop, I had a call from Dan, who now has to consider their options, bless him – Archie due for 'mask fitting' for radiotherapy tomorrow the 23rd – his 2nd birthday. They hope to get results tomorrow too. What a hard time they are having. I said we'd go out asap. as they need Geordie & Thierry looking after – he was very pleased. Now I can hear loud waterfalls or a stream running off the slabs in the distance, nearby the bubbling flow, singing along and I have heard voices (In the dark, I listen to the varied pitch of the river sounds and imagine voices – perhaps people from the past!). Still light, but time to snuggle down – again cool.

Day 119. 23/7 Loch an Nid to Inverlael

Broomfield Holiday Park, Ullapool	15 miles
Wet start, slowly improving through day	2818 ft

A wet start that dried up as we walked, to finish with a bright evening in Ullapool. We took a taxi from Inverlael to Ullapool as it is off route.

A very windy, squally night and rain. Lay awake thinking the fly sheet might split!

Up at 6, and away just before 8 – another slippy, plodgy walk alongside the loch with wind and rain squalls in our backs. Very dramatic mountain land all around, An Teallach very dark and spewing clouds.

Aghainn Loch an Nid

We reached the stony track and had a long plod slowly up and up, An Teallach to our left, the massive, dark, jagged ridge emerging from the clouds. Shenavall Bothy low down in the glen:

Not a soul about, until we were over the bealach and nearer Corrie Hallie. Here we called in at the craft shop hoping for tea in the porch again. Aida and Brian[*] still there, she so quick speaking and expressive (American), and he more quiet and introvert, but he came out to chat with us. A very welcome cuppa tea and cake.

Leaving An Teallach behind as we head to Loch Broom

Still 5 miles to go, up and over an old track contouring the hillside, gently rising up and up, very boggy as usual. In the end, I just splosh through the lot, tiring though.

We finally look down on the end of Loch Broom and the main valley and road into Ullapool. Had to walk a mile on it, with traffic zooming by fast, to reach Inverlael, where we phoned for a taxi to Ullapool, off route. A very friendly local lady came in a Diablo van, £12.50 for all of us.

Windy on the campsite, but we had a reliable marine forecast from Brian for improving weather, so pitched right on the shore.

* Aida runs a lovely craft shop and Brian runs the Summer Isles Tour boat. We first met when we called in with Barney on our Cape Wrath trek.

Fabulous sunset, stunning to watch the light and try to paint. Slept well, to the sound of wind and waves.

Sun setting over the Summer Isles

Day 120. 24/7 Ullapool Rest Day 1

Rainy, lazy start, felt very relaxed and didn't stir until 9am!

Washing done, took Barney to vet for a check up, no problem now thankfully, and got more anti inflammatory Loxicom just in case needed. Vet said he'd donate to our Guide Dogs.

Bob got his blog done – day became sunny and all the tops clear and beautiful light on the water. Noisy kids on campsite at 10pm.

Card 16 25/7 Ullapool	Doh I can't do blue sea & skies! Sitting outside tent in sun, no midges, summer Isles on horizon. I just PAINTED the Calmac ferry!! & nearly added a ladies rowing team who just rowed by!! Having lazy day today before final push to the 'summit' top! Another 10 days to go. Over some ground covered be4 – Oykel Bridge, Ben More Assynt, the Crask Inn & N. East to coast. Lovely to talk on phone yesterday. Hard to imagine, getting home (somehow!) & then flying off to Oz so soon – oh well! Lots Love Jos & Team Barney xxx
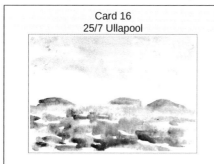	

Day 121. 25/7 Ullapool Rest Day 2

Lazing about in sun, NW breeze. Had a wander round the village – very tempting bookshops. Funny, but not interested in food, eating out.

Had a plateful of pasta and mushroom sauce in a pub last night – it was enough for 2 meals!

The first campsite in 12 days

Not much to do today, surrounded by stuff to pack for last leg of our long walking journey.

Summer Isles sunset from the tent

We 'bumped into' Noana again in Ullapool. She was so pleased and happy she had walked Kinlochewe to Sheneval Bothy and then to Inverlael – by herself! Good on her.

Arrived in Ullapool by taxi! It's not actually on the trail so we don't have to walk it which is just as well as it's a terrible road.

We've had a hard time since Fort William with wet and windy weather making it a struggle at times. Still enjoyed it though, linking up lots of areas we have walked in previously.

Kinlochewe was our first shop for a long time, and now at Ullapool we have a campsite and a Tesco's. We're spending an extra day here as the weather has improved and we want a rest. Barney is enjoying doing nothing.

I'll try and post a selection of pics but it's proving difficult this far north – the phone data connection can't handle it so I have had to resort to WiFi in a pub – life is so hard…

Ticks

Ticks are now an ever present potential health threat when walking in most parts of the country, mostly in bracken and grassy and wooded areas especially in the Scottish Highlands, the Pennines and Northumberland – all high ground! Whether from sheep, deer or other animals they can easily be picked up by both humans and dogs. They 'wait' on plant growth, for a host to pass and attach to the host in order to extract blood as a source of food. The host is often unaware of the attached tick as it injects a powerful anaesthetic at the point of connection.

Ticks can be the cause of a range of problems including Lyme disease which can be very hazardous to both humans and dogs if left untreated. Dogs can be protected from ticks with drops applied to their coat at regular intervals and this was the case with Barney. Humans however have no equivalent protection.

The recommended procedure to avoid infection, which we followed, is to regularly check skin for attached ticks. Removing ticks within 24 hours of attachment, or preferably earlier, makes it unlikely that Lyme disease will be contracted.

We always carry a tick remover, don't wear shorts and kept socks tucked over trousers, at ankles. We wore Goretex 'wet gear' most days anyway.

Jos regularly checked Barney and we'd get the tick removers out quickly if any found.

Days 120-121 Rest days in Ullapool

We needed to resupply and visit the vets in Ullapool so decided on two days to give us a chance to recover. Ullapool was sunny and not too many midges – bliss!

Day 122. 26/7 Inverlael to Knockdamph

Knockdamph Bothy	11.5 miles
Sunny start, warm and dry all day	2108 ft

Taxi back to Inverlael and off we go for the final section of the trek across to John o' Groats which is still about 130 miles away!

This was another section of the Cape Wrath trail which is new to us, as we went a different way before. Fine initially but then very hard going on a long trackless section before we reached Loch an Daimh and the bothy at Knockdamph.

Surprise at the bothy – a fire was alight. A man and his two sons were staying for a few days, so the bothy was dry and warm.

Sunny morning, no wind, no midges. Plenty of time to pack up, as taxi not due till 9am, to take us back to where we 'left off' at Inverlael.

Some of the mountains surrounding us

It was a hard day – first through forest on tracks rising uphill, in HOT sun, then the track on to the open hill gave way to boggy 4 wheel drive tracks through peat. Stunning panoramas of mountain ranges – Ben Dearg, Fannichs, Fisherfield, An Teallach.

Looking back to An Teallach after the long ascent

The route grew more challenging underfoot as we made our way downhill to cross the River Douchery – slipping and sliding.

The Cape Wrath Trail isn't obvious in places

Had a break by the river, perfect camping spots but a long way still to go, the worst bit to come, following the river on rough pathless ground. Up and down and round, till it turned into a gorge with a narrow deer track to the side to balance along.

I was tired and just had to grit my teeth and keep going, I do find the slippy, muddy, no path sections slow – I'm slow!

Eventually we reached Loch Damph – phew, about 4:30 so 7 hours of walking, then a stony track by the loch to reach Knockdamph Bothy. Found it occupied by 2 boys and their dad. Oakley, Dylan & Anthony, who lived near John o' Groats.

Fire lit ready for us

They were very friendly and welcoming, and a lovely fire going so we had cups of tea and a good chat. We moved into the downstairs room where I write this now on the sleeping bench using head torch as it's a bit dark for a change.

Bothies

Bothies are 'simple shelters in remote country for the use & benefit of all who love wild & lonely places' as stated on the Mountain Bothies Association (MBA) website. Often they used to be home to a shepherd and his family. We have stayed in or camped next to many bothies over the years and being an MBA member, receive the regular newsletter from the association.

Knockdamph Bothy

Bothies have already been mentioned with Greg's Hut (page 180) being a good place to spend the night in bad weather in the Pennines and Maol-bhuide (page 271) a well placed bothy in a remote location. An entry about us in the newsletter published before we started the trip resulted in our meeting with another member at Killin earlier in the trip (page 235).

Knockdamph Bothy is unusual as it has an upstairs bedroom that contains a bed. We first stayed here on the last section of the Cape Wrath trail which was our first long distance hike with Barney in 2009. We took the upstairs room and started unpacking. A little while later we heard the downstairs door open and a man with his husky came in (also wearing dog panniers). After introductions, we returned to the upstairs bedroom to continue sorting out our stuff. Barney disappeared unnoticed and suddenly we heard a terrible commotion downstairs – a dog fight! He had decided the husky was an unwelcome visitor and stood his ground. Luckily, the owner managed to part the dogs by the time we had descended (rapidly).

Our friend Wendy (who we walked with earlier from Fort William and features again in this book) had stopped briefly at the bothy recently and made an entry in the logbook. We knew the husky owner was a fast walker and so Jos gave him a note to pass onto Wendy should he catch her up. It was addressed – 'Wendy, long, 'silver' hair, Paramo clothing and a sheep dog Meg. She was amazed when a stranger, stopped to give her the note, saying "Are you Wendy?" Sometime later, Wendy wrote this up, sent it into TGO (The Great Outdoors) magazine and won a bottle of whisky for the Letter of the Month!

Day 123. 27/7 Knockdamph to River Oykel

Wild camp near Salachy by the River Oykel	13.5 miles
Grey, warm, muggy with rain in the evening	1090 ft

We had all been this way before but the plus this time was that the bar at the Oykel Bridge Hotel was open. Sandwiches and soft drinks were readily consumed while we listened to the fishermen's talk before they all went off for an afternoons fishing.

On the track down to Oykel Bridge, a cattle grid is well known to us – the last time here the adjoining gate was locked so we were deciding how to get Barney across. Jos walked across to see if she could find a gap in the fence and Barney decided to follow by jumping over the grid. Needless to say he didn't make it and his legs went down between the bars! Luckily nothing was broken, just a grazed shin and he had to be lifted out. Fortunately, this time, the padlock had gone so an easy gate.

We're now camped in Glen Oykel having had a hard day getting to Knockdamph bothy yesterday where we were greeted by a roaring fire (it was occupied already)!

Sitting in tent after tea, rain pattering down. River Oykel bubbling along close by – very close, we are perched on a narrow tent space piece of grass on the river bank, where we camped 6 years ago!

Meeting up with old friends

Left the Bothy this morning thinking Bob had lost his mobile. He had everything out of his rucksack to search for it. When we finally got going, he found it in the most obvious place – the phone holder on his shoulder strap!

Today was a lot of hard surface tracks, I felt for Barney as he kept trying for softer ground. First the hard track on and on to Oykel Bridge through trees – all very quiet re. bird song now.

The cattle grid where we previously had a close shave with Barney

We were very glad to find the Oykel Bridge Hotel Bar open at lunchtime. We had juice, pot of tea, parsnip and thyme soup and very generous ham salad sarnies. Had a pud too – bit much – rhubarb and orange crumble. There was enough for 2 on my plate. Phew, couldn't leave any though.

Well fortified, we continued on the track we'd walked before above the River Oykel, through an estate with 'free ranging bulls, cows and calves' - grey, big horned ones. The track was just as long as last time, our bags feeling 'end of the day' heavy. Very glad to get to a cattle grid out of cow estate and to find our little camping spot on the bank still here.

Painting in the tent when 'midgy' outside

A good fishing pool was full of ghyllies and clients earlier.

River Oykel

Tomorrow, the same route as the Cape Wrath Trail, till we reach Ben More Assynt when we veer in a NE direction, heading for our destination. How do we feel? Mixed, with Australian trip ahead, no time to unwind, recap – well not at home. I like this walking life = no worries, they have to go on hold, while we get on with the business – the tent routine morning and night. The days walk, concentrating on path, feet, today a plod on hard track, don't think much, just finding tunes in my head to match the pole rhythm, look and listen for birds.

BIRDSONG noted up the country so far –

- Cornwall – sea birds
- Devon – returning Warblers in the woods
- Somerset and Exmoor hills – Larks and Pippets
- Somerset levels – Sedge and reed warblers
- Somewhere, swallows, martins and swifts return.
- Dawn chorus – 4am wake
- Offa's Dyke, Shropshire, Midlands – Woodland birds
- Derbyshire and Pennines – Curlew, snipe, golden plover and lapwing (moorland birds)
- Scotland, Highlands – Buzzard, sandpiper, oyster catcher, red throated diver, warblers stopped singing, lots pippets

Flowers

- Cornwall – Violets, primroses, daffs – March / April
- Nenthead – daffs in June!
- Tees – Globe flowers, pink primroses, gentian, loads of meadow flowers
- Scotland – Marsh orchids galore
- End July – Grasses seeding, purple thistle, purple Belladonna

Day 124. 28/7 River Oykel to Creag Riabhach

Wild camp north east of Ben More Assynt	16 miles
Cool with rain at times	2231 ft

Wet to start again. Another very remote section of the walk as we traversed around the flanks of Ben More Assynt and headed towards Loch Shin. The route followed an old track and then we decided to leave it and follow hydro tracks to avoid what I thought might be a difficult river crossing, but when we arrived, having detoured several miles, the water level was very low.

Midge nets on at our River Oykel campsite

Very midgy damp start. Must have rained a lot in night as the River Oykel is very swollen and noisy.

We were away by 8 am and made our way along the track, ignored a sign saying CW Trail, directing you into the forest. We kept by the riverbank following a quad bike 'line', eventually joining the forest track further up which turned into hard surface. Luckily we

294

were all to one side, as a ghyllie came round a bend in a fast car not expecting pedestrians! The track led down to Loch Ailsh, with the building Benmore Lodge at its head. We followed the track behind the Lodge and after 2 ½ hours, we finally stopped for a break, looking up the Oykel valley and Ben More Assynt all shrouded in cloud, very dramatic.

River Oykel and Ben More Assynt

Just got a painting done when the rain started in earnest, we had it head on, taking a different track to the CW Trail this time, and heading NE following the Allt Sail an Ruathair stream. Very plodgy and I got wet feet straight away crossing streams:

Barney watching Jos is safe across

Bob very pessimistic re. our chances of crossing the River Cassley later. He can be so doom and gloom these days! *(Bob: warnings in guidebooks about it being impassable after rain. This area has the least used O.S. map – not many people come here!)*

The path was rough and old, an overgrown cart track and we had a steep grind up the shoulder of Meall an Aonaich (Eagle Rock). Then it was plodging through peat bog, but still the old way occasionally showing through. We stopped for lunch by a loch but not for long as feeling cold. Kept going until we came to a stone track running in a SE direction. Bob decided 'too risky' to try and cross the River Cassley further up, so we had to slog in the OPPOSITE direction to where we wanted to go for 3k and then north, following a big metal pipe leading to a bridge over the river and a power station.

View back to Ben More Assynt, looking for a dry spot to camp

Safely across the benign looking river, we found the track leading us back NW along the River Cassley to a point where it looked possible to cross after all! However, we were now higher up on the side of the glen, on trackless ground. We decided to make for the bealach and look for somewhere less boggy to pitch. I found running water and some semi flat ground, with a view back to many lochans in the glen at the foot of Ben More Assynt. Here we are, 'in the middle of nowhere', warmed up and full up after our meal, me writing, dog fast asleep using my leg as a pillow and Bob stretched out after cooking.

A boggy camp for the night after crossing a very wet area

I can hear a spring and burn 'glugging away' in the distance. No wind tonight and too cold for midges. Another long day, 16 rough miles but felt fine as cool weather.

Day 125. 29/7 Creag Riabhach to Crask Inn

Crask Inn room	15.8 miles
Generally dry, cool and grey	1556 ft

Heading for a pub! We've wanted to stay at this inn – one famous amongst walkers and fishermen alike. Situated in the middle of a large expanse of remote country, it was quite a walk to get to it. The ground was very wet and although we could see it in the distance, it took several hours of hard walking, including a difficult stream crossing to arrive.

Am sitting in bed in a warm room, socks all drying on radiator.

Another long walk from our pitch on the bealach, down to Loch Shin, we took nearly 2 hours, on all sodden, slippery ground and peat hags. It was a relief to reach a track, leading to a bridge and the 'main' A838 road from Lairg to Durness.

When walking along the roadside, Bob got a phone call from Dan in Australia who wanted to talk to his dad about the decision they had to take – whether Archie should have a course of radiotherapy. What a place to be – our Oz family the other side of the world, going through such trauma, and us hiking along a deserted road alongside Loch Shin in Sutherland. Later, Dan sent Bob a 'flow chart' of stats re. the pros and cons of radiotherapy and Archie's chances of survival.

We left the road to take a forest track running parallel. Later, on exit, there was a very high gate to climb. Luckily, we found Barney a way under the fence. We came out back on to the A838 briefly at Fiag Bridge, then came the 'hard bit'.

Deer fences can be a problem to get the dog through – luckily this one had a gap for Barney but not us

In showery rain, we cut across country to reach the Crask Inn. There were no paths, very boggy, and deep burns to cross. First a slog uphill from where we could could see the Inn far off in the distance. I spotted G&W's campervan on the road at 3:45pm, looking like a 'Dinky Toy'!

298

A distant Crask Inn – didn't look far but took 2 hours to reach

It took us 2 hours or more to reach the Inn. Felt exhausted. Got very wet crossing the last burn – it was very deep and fast flowing. Barney even got carried along by the flow and Bob had to help him out!

A massive pot of tea revived me. We are in the bunkhouse, have our own room and the radiator is on so everything is drying out.

Bunkhouse on the left, Inn on the right

Lovely meal in the Inn and now G&W poring over maps with us – they'll be with us to the End.

Blog Notes for Days 124,125

Some serious off road walking to get to the Crask Inn. All the ground is saturated making walking difficult especially on the pathless sections.

A couple of good wild camps, one being in a really remote spot east of Ben More Assynt.

The Inn is wonderful – our first bed in nearly 4 weeks and electric lights.

Geoff & Wendy are with us again and are helping out with our last stages. Wendy will be walking with us in a few days and we can reduce our carrying loads which is a real bonus.

I'll try posting a few pictures – if nothing appears it hasn't worked!

Staying in Touch

Our plan was to stay in touch with family and friends using our mobile phones as required. Initially a convenience. After news of Archie's predicament, they became a vital part of the trek. Mobile 'smart' phones meant we could keep up-to-date on his situation whilst continuing the walk knowing that if our help was required we could change plans.

Direct calls, texts, emails and phone apps including Blogger and Facebook Messenger used, mostly by Bob, whenever conditions allowed. Until we reached the Scottish Highlands phone coverage was normally adequate – if no coverage at one place, then it would not normally be long before we moved on to find a decent mobile signal. Once into the Highlands however this became more problematic and in several places we had no contact for several days

Day 126. 30/7 Crask Inn to Loch Choire

Wild camp next to Loch Choire	6.7 miles
Dry day, grey to start but fine later	597 ft

As well as staying at a pub, we have met up with friends Geoff & Wendy from Arisaig, who we last saw on the stage from Fort William, where Geoff took our bags and Wendy walked with us for the day. They are now taking most of our food so we only need carry supplies until we meet them again in two days.

We stopped early at Loch Choire – it's a lovely spot and we are definitely feeling tired after the last few days, all of which have been hard.

Lie in after late night and getting up in the night – beer?

Sorted stuff leaving loads in the box as G&W taking it, only need 1 meal before we meet up again. Fine start and so far, writing this in the evening, <u>dry all day</u> for once.

Bealach Easach reached and view of Loch a Bhealaich

We left the Crask Inn, heading east on an old track which took us up to the Bealach Easach and then down past high crags.

Didn't spot the eagle Mike the landlord had talked of though. Both feeling very weary after days of effort, so when we reached an idyllic spot, the sandy, grassy edge of Loch Choire; we stopped at 3:30pm.

Very peaceful, and after tea and the whisky Mike had given us in a plastic bottle, Bruachladdich (Islay) malt! I slept an hour.

Now totally still and midges out – doh. I've collected drift wood for a beach fire but we'll see if the midges are too bad.

Loch Choire and home for the night

Thoughts of poor Dan struggling with decision re. Archie's treatment, radiotherapy / survival rates on our minds as we walked. He sent us a flow chart he'd written of pros and cons, which we read on Bob's phone in the Inn.

Loch Choire by campfire

I did get a good fire going – fish plopping in the still water, deer barking deeply from within the nearby trees – annoyed we were on their patch? Such a beautiful spot to camp.

Light rain began to fall as I went to bed. Whisky kept my head awake grrrr…

Loch Choire sunset and rain

Day 127. 31/7 Loch Choire to Kinbrace

Wild camp next to railway line, Kinbrace	20.8 miles
Grey with some rain to start, brighter later	1324 ft

We arranged to meet Geoff & Wendy part way through today's trek and then Wendy walked with us while Geoff took the sacks – what a man!
After a lovely walk around the loch where we saw divers close to, we then had a 10 mile trudge along a land rover track – very remote with spacious views. Wendy joined us for the last 5 or so miles to Kinbrace where we camped next to the railway line.

What a long day.

We started at 7:50 and it looked fine, so no over-trousers on for the first time in weeks. But rain began lightly as we approached an estate bothy by Loch Choire, so we went in and got the wet gear on. Looked a very well equipped bothy. Good walk on lakeside track, through trees, all very pleasant. Saw 2 divers close to the bank; grey throated – black and white stripy backs. Once past the estate buildings at end of the loch, we veered off on an old track on the hillside. Didn't last long as we came to a padlocked, new deer fence gate, grrrr, so made our way down to the estate road and began the long slog on a hardish surface to Badanloch Lodge 6-7 miles away where we were to meet G&W in their van.

Hard going. Good views of Ben Loyal and possibly Ben Hope – lots of space and remote lochs.

We had mobile signal in the middle of nowhere! I had a chat with Lorraine as I walked along. She was in Reading and told me "1000 people have signed up for 'Match a Mile for Barney' and one woman's raised £1000. All thanks to you guys!"

On and on we plodded, till at last the cream campervan was a dot in the green!

Later, revived with tea and sarnies with G&W, before setting off again for Kinbrace, but without our heavy sacks. A forest had been felled since the guide book was written and we had fences to climb over and under before we could get going. The terrain was quite tussocky as we contoured round the hill above the road.

No sacks and easy walking

The sun came out and I could have had a go at painting – clouds, shafts of light, rain, golden grass, blue hills. However, we had to press on, past Kinbrace, following the river till we reached Geoff at 7:45pm.

Phew. Now pitched by the rail line, a train to Thurso just gone by. Geese honking, as they fly overhead, snipe whickering and rain pattering on tent. Oh, saw a Golden Eagle today, – huge wings and 'fingers'.

Day 128. 1/8 Kinbrace to Dail Righe

Wild camp at Dail Righe, River Thurso	14.2 miles
Generally dry ending in sunshine and showers	1293 ft

Wendy and her dog, Meg, came part of the way for this one and it immediately started hard. We have found that forestry and other changes in Scotland has meant the route details have been outdated in some instances – this was one of them. A struggle to get through what should have been an easy stretch made hard by a new forestry plantation. This was followed by a big climb and then miles of peat hags mixed with waterlogged ground. The trig point at the top stands on a mound of peat which is slowly being eroded, eventually it will fall over. Then followed a long land rover track and finally we reached our camping spot for the night, quite a relief.

100 days of actual walking.

Another long day and I found it hard, and got cross and tired with all the rough terrain. We started off with Wendy and Meg over rough ground, newly planted with trees. There were fences to climb over, until we reached the moorland heading up to Knockfin Heights. That was steep, climbing up the side of Knockfin Burn. Here Wendy left us to return to Geoff and the van. On the summit it was a sea of peat hags we had to step across, like boulder hopping. We were lucky to have a fine day for it, it would have been much worse in wet weather.

Ben Hope and Ben Loyal from Knockfin Heights ascent

At LAST reached the trig. point of Knockfin Heights. Views of stormy skies west to Ben Loyal and beyond, north to dear Hoy and Rackwick cliffs[*], to the east, rose a steep looking mountain, Morven. A grand view.

Knockfin Heights trig. point

[*] We have got to know Hoy – Orkney's high island very well after many visits over the years, one being our honeymoon in 1976.

Food keeps dog awake while Jos paints.

I tried a painting or two, before more tortuous stumbling across the plateaux on a compass bearing, having to detour round mires, and crevasse like peat ditches.

West to Ben Griam Mòr and Griam Beg with Ben Loyal behind cloud

We followed a stream, I was hardly putting one foot in front of the other. Bob took some of my weight. Finally, reached a hard track, what a relief but of course then it was hard on the feet etc.

A track at last; Morven in the distance

We followed it for miles, leaving the mountains behind as we headed east, past a keepers place, The Glutt and on and on. Both very sore and tired till around 6, reached flat ground at Dail Righe by the River Thurso:

Pitch at Dail Righe

Just got our tent up before a heavy shower, then sunshine – had door of tent open 10 mins. before midges. Tea over, we listened to 'Take the Floor' on Radio Scotland* as it's Saturday night, good reception too. Today felt too much after yesterday.

* We usually do this at home, before Ceili House on Irish RTE Radio 1

Day 129. 2/8 Dail Righe to A9

Watten Caravan Park	14.9 miles
Sunshine and warmer	346 ft

> More track, and eventually we met up with Geoff & Wendy again. Wendy & Meg to join us for the walk whilst Geoff did the transport. Jos had described the camper van previously as the (n)ice cream van as it is cream coloured so Geoff & Wendy presented us with... ice creams!
>
> The destination was the A9 but we weren't camping on it. Geoff picked us up and we made our way to the Watten campsite – not the best one of our trip. The walking was good however, apart from Jos dropping her Australian cap and we having to return (in the camper van) to find it.

A better day re. length of walk, although still a long day. Left at 8:20am in SUNSHINE – no gaiters and no over-trousers. Warm walking along the track – 2 hours later, we reached the beach...

Loch More and time for a paddle

Loch More. Really nice to sit, paddle even, then sketch and eat a flapjack. Just about to leave, when G&W and dog Meg turned up, so we walked together back to the (N)ICE CREAM campervan and lo and behold 4 ice creams!

Ice creams in the shade

They really are our Guardian Angels of the end of the End to End!

We had our sandwiches and tea in the van, then Wendy came with us to walk the next leg of about 10k to the A9 to meet Geoff. We followed the winding River Thurso on a fair track for a change, I unwittingly dropped my cap on a steep section where I slipped and we found it later – hooray! I'm very 'attached' to it, well normally. So pleased I found it. It's my Australian one.

Card 17	The last of the mountains west – from Loch More Caithness. Saw an osprey before painting this, then Geoff & Wendy & Meg met us! & Wendy & Meg joined us for the afternoon walk. All sitting (sleeping dogs) in their campervan now drinking T!! before we hike on to the coast Keiss – Final day tomorrow! Hard to believe. Seen Hoy already from hilltops – this is last card unless I do an extra!! xxxx
 Sunday 2/8	

The 'way' led through old sand 'quarries' then we waded through long grass till we found a place to ford the little river. Geoff and van were not far away, just off the A9, where we start again tomorrow.

They drove us to the campsite near Watten where we are now – 9pm and on pudding stage of our tea. Again rain started as we put the tent up. Heavy now. Wick to Thurso main road nearby.

Saw Hoy again today. Feel a bit sad we won't be going there after we've finished, but as Wendy pointed out, we didn't have to give up the walk.

I wonder when we will go out to Australia.

Penultimate day tomorrow.

Oh, saw OSPREY close-up! It took off from the river bank just as we approached. Saw another later, or same one, flying.

Day 130. 3/8 A9 to Keiss

Wild camp next to Keiss beach	17 miles
Wet start, improving through the day	496 ft

A full day for Wendy & Meg. First forest, then steadily down to Watten where we enjoyed our first shop since Ullapool.

Next was a change of route – Andy Robinson in the guide describes the crossing of the Moss of Killimster as hard – if he says that, he means hard! Given that it is hard because of the let's say, damp nature of the terrain and the fact that everywhere is already waterlogged this year and we'd had steady rain last night, we decided to bite the bullet and walk the road instead. Barney really slows up on roads normally but having Meg along made all the difference and he trotted along at normal speed.

Eventually we left the road and headed for the beach. This was the East coast and our first sea en route since Devon although we had camped next to Loch Broom at Ullapool.

Geoff had spotted a fish & chip van in Keiss earlier where we finished so we raced off in anticipation, to find it had shut 10 minutes earlier! Yet another dehydrated meal it was then...

Pouring rain to pack up – hooray Bob agreed best to leave Watten campsite and find a pitch at Keiss. Geoff took us back to the A9 spot we left off yesterday and we walked along, luckily on a grass verge, but what a start! Lots of rain and wash off fast lorries zooming past.

We soon turned into a forest by an open gate. Good sandy track to march along till Bob said "This is where we climb the fence, using an oil drum" (written in the Guide book).

Oil drum used to get over deer fence which is mentioned in Andy's guide

Once again Wendy and I doing assault course tactics, wobbling over the wire. The dogs crawled under where there was a ditch.

A stretch of grassy, tussocky ground before a deserted farm and a lot of shorn (Sean the) sheep. A farm / tarmac track took us over flat land, reminding us of Somerset Levels, with cows in fields. Quite a trog, before the road led to Watten. Such contrast in landscape to yesterdays walking by the River Thurso, leaving the mountains.

Watten shop was open, so dog food and bars etc. Our first shop since Ullapool. Geoff turned up and gave us a cup of tea in the van!

Next leg was a long 7-8 miles on tarmac, minor roads bar one, to avoid The Moss – difficult says Andy R = v. hard / extreme in these wet conditions. So we passed time chatting and Meg set a good pace for Barney. Such a help.

We don't quite manage 20mph

We were so relieved to leave a busy fast road and continue on a quiet one, till eventually we turned off at a pipeline works and onto the dunes, **<u>arriving at the coast at last.</u>** The dogs gambled about and we had a paddle in the freezing sea to ease aching feet!

The sea again but this time it's the east coast

Good old Geoff was there at a car park – more tea.

Our penultimate campsite of the trek, at Keiss

We pitched the tent on a footpath above the beach and cooked, missing the view as all doors closed against midges.

Sinclair's Bay, Keiss

Now there is a thundering roar, like a continuous waterfall, it's high tide and nearby, waves continuously rolling in and breaking. It's completely calm now but 40mph winds forecast for tomorrow – could be epic on our last day!

Wendy asked 'What was most memorable part of the trip?' The best / The worst? Memorable people? So many memories to recall.[*]

* We eventually put together some comments on this – see page 331

316

Day 131. 4/8 Keiss to John o' Groats

John o' Groats Campsite	13.5 miles	
Bright and Breezy with glorious end to the day	1591 ft	

Well, what a final day!

The guidebook describes this as not suitable for children or dogs and we had two – I'll let you decide who they are...

A glorious walk along cliff edges where sometimes you hang onto the fence because the drop is so close! The 40mph winds never really happened – it was just a classic windy coastal walk with the wind in the right direction.

We met up with Geoff at a couple of points which helped progress a lot, hot drinks and food. Again, our heavy sacks were in the van and Barney carried nothing, he loved it.

Then, after a long day, we arrived at John O' Groats and... surprise, surprise, Kay, Nigel and Guide dog Jackie appeared at the end! They'd travelled all the way up from Falmouth to greet us. They saw us off at Land's End and I remember Nigel saying 'we might get up to John o' Groats to greet you' but never really expected it, as it is a 900 mile trip (don't we know). He even posted Facebook posts to make it look as though they were still at home. What a finish – even the sun was shining!

Last Day.

Up early, very breezy. Thought 40mph wind forecast, so got tent down quick and sat in the van while G&W got breakfast over. Set off at 8:45 for a scramble along Keiss beach stones, to the harbour, then along to Keiss Castle.

Keiss Castle

From there we had quite hard walking in long uneven grass with field fences to our left and cliff drops to our right, plus a few fences to climb over / under.

We met Geoff at a car park for coffee and then more cliffs, walking round long geos, an ancient castle precariously built atop a stack.

Stacks on the way to Freswick Bay

<u>Stunning day</u> with cliffs, birds, white crashing waves, blue sky, blue sea. A real treat for our last day. Another welcome meet up with Geoff at Freswick Bay for lunch, our last one. On to Skirza Head, and easy walking on heathery turf via Skippie and Wife Geos up to Duncansby Stacks – very jagged, pointy, rocky stacks, next came Duncansby Head and lighthouse. I made time to paint.

The Stacks of Duncansby and a very Cornish like coastline

Again found Geoff at a car park with the NICE CREAM VAN! and cup of tea ready, before the last 1 ½ miles along the N. COAST to the John o' Groats buildings. It only started to sink in then, seeing the familiar building, that we had no more walking north to do – we'd turned the corner, reached the end!

Duncansby Head and the last trig. point

Lovely sunny evening, and so surprised to find Kay and Nigel and guide dog Jackie waiting for us, having driven up from Falmouth to greet us!

Well I never! A surprise greeting from Kay and Nigel last seen at Land's End.

We had lots of pictures taken at the signpost by Robert, a friendly photographer from Wick. "We looked euphoric and very brown" said Lorraine from Dogs Unite when she saw the photo!

Photo by Robert MacDonald, Northern Studios, Wick

On to the bar at the hotel for meal with G&W, Kay & Nigel, and Jackie came too.

We said our goodbyes – quite sad to see G&W go. We forgot to sign the E to E book! What a cheerful pair and what a help they have been to support us at the end of our long walk with Meg of course and the nice cream van.

Bob & I late to bed (in the tent, not the hotel!), looking at messages coming in.

Day 132. 5/8 John o' Groats camp day

A rest day.
The weather stayed fine so we simply... chilled out.
We finished by visiting the Seaview Hotel and I had quite the best seafood meal I have ever had!

Lovely sunny start, a walk to the shop. Had a chat with a Mr Moat and now writing in tent.

Looking at Orkney feeling a little sorry we aren't going over[*] – especially as so close but they'll be there for another trip next year. Dan & Sal will be glad of our help. The depths of winter there. Oh dear, never mind, just think of what they are going through.

Now to paint the Pentland Firth while I'm here, colours changing, rain due.

Last painting – Stroma and raindrops

* Originally, our intention was to travel onto Hoy in Orkney where we have friends

Day 133. 6/8 Going home – south

A 6 O'clock taxi to Thurso station for the 6:50 to Inverness. Then it was trains to Edinburgh, Carlisle and finally Haltwhistle where Sue picked us up – thanks.
Before we knew where we were, we were having a meal in our local, the Crown in Catton and that's almost it...

Wet, windy night, little sleep. Up at 5am as taxi at 6. Grey, wet morning, we were in Thurso for 6:30! Time to walk Barney before long day on trains, Thurso – Inverness via our wild camp near Kinbrace, flat featureless bog land. East to Helmsdale on the coast, inland to Lairg then Beauly and Dingwall.

Déjà vu? Barney with us back on a train heading south

Mountains now and on to Aviemore (next train) and A9 route – Drumochter Pass and Blair Atholl – Perth, Kirkaldy, Edinburgh. The Virgin train was a blur as we sped down to Carlisle.

Then the more sedate Tyne Valley Line – to be met by an excited Sue[*] at Halty[†] who drove us home.

Warmer than when we left in March. Photo by Sue Dunne

Hudsriding looked so nice and welcoming, tidy and clean and clear of clutter – like a holiday home. We soon messed it up!

Thank you Lucy and Batch

* Sue, another local friend.
† Halty – local name for Haltwhistle.

Notes

- Total days 131
- 102 days walking
- 1330 miles walked
- 180,278 ft ascended

Nights at:

- Campsite: 67
- Wild camping: 29
- Interludes (Dorset & home): 16
- Friends & Family: 11
- Bothies: 3
- Inns: 5

Total Raised for Guide Dogs

- By Barney: £8000
- By Match a Mile for Barney: Greater than £22000[*]
- Total: Over **£30000!**

* Money continued to be collected long after the trip finished

Blog

The blog can be found at: barneyslongwalk.blogspot.com/ and includes various pages detailing the trip.

The blog was updated using the Google Blogger mobile app. This generally worked fine when we had good, fast phone coverage or wifi. It was unreliable where coverage only gave low level data transfer such as in the Scottish Highlands[*]

Facebook

The 'BarneysLongWalk' Facebook page has been renamed 'Adventures with Monty' but it still includes all the original posts. It can be found at www.facebook.com/AdventuresWithMonty/

Facebook was kept up-to-date using the Facebook Page Manager mobile app. This worked fine and would recover well from connection failures, dropouts and other connection issues.

Guidebooks

The guides we used in 2015 included:

- The End to End Trail (Cicerone) by Andy Robinson.

- SWCP Association notes on the trail in reverse.

- Offa's Dyke Path South

- The Pennine Way (Cicerone) by Paddy Dillon

All were cut up so we only carried route details.

Cicerone also now have guides for the SWCP and Offa's Dyke National Trails and a 2nd edition of the End to End Trail with updated route details.

The Limestone Way, St Cuthbert's Way and the Southern Upland Way also have guidebooks which can be useful for planning.

---

* Using Vodafone which has limited data coverage in the Highlands

What happened next

We had a few (10) days at home, a welcoming party at our local pub – the Crown, Catton (thanks to Pippa from Guide Dogs) where we were surprised to see Nikki from Scottish Guide Dogs down for the afternoon!

Who has Barney for the next
3 months

Most of the 10 days were spent sorting out a trip to Australia to help with Dan and family for 3 months while Archie had ongoing treatment. No time to think about what we had just accomplished. We had to get Barney re-homed for a while – fortunately friends Jane & Neil were prepared to take him on at short notice, which made it much easier for us. Family and friends were able to cover the times when this proved a problem.

Lucy & Batch, our house sitters for the trek were able to stay for another 3 months in the house while we were away again, solving what would otherwise would have been a difficult problem.

Leaving Barney for 3 months

Archie in hospital

We arrived in Australia at the end of the southern winter – everybody seemed to have coughs and colds! Dan, Sally and boys were in Melbourne for a few days whilst Archie had another dose of chemotherapy treatment. This was part of the routine they had and we settled into – chemo in Melbourne, a few days at home and then Archie went downhill from the chemo, picking up infections, resulting in a stay in the local hospital in Albury. This happened on a regular basis after every chemo treatment. Anybody that has had chemotherapy probably knows the score.

I (Bob) went down with a bad cough / cold* almost as soon as we had arrived in Oz – it was still cold and Australian houses are not well insulated.†

We bought road bikes to get out once or twice a week and managed a few trips away to the hills when it was possible – the change from backpacking in Scotland to helping look after two young boys in a small house was difficult to cope with at first, but our problems were minor compared with those Dan & Sally faced.

One year on...

We left Australia hopeful that Archie was over the worst. The following April however proved otherwise – his tumour had re-appeared. Dan, Sally and the boys had to move to Melbourne for a year whilst Archie went through a more aggressive treatment schedule‡ – how they coped, I don't know, the previous year was bad enough. Fortunately they had great support from the local community where they live. Even Dan's employer at the Jindera Hotel kept his job on hold as head chef while they were away. Their

* Probably caught on the 'plane over.
† Dan & Sal live in Jindera, a village north of Albury Wodonga, 3 hours drive from Melbourne.
‡ At Melbourne Royal Children's Hospital.

friends also raised funds to help out with what was obviously a difficult financial situation. This is where a local supportive, community can really make a difference.

Our walking trips returned to normal with occasional multi-day expeditions in Scotland* along with local walks in the Pennines and Lake District.

We had cause to travel south (a rarity for us) after we were invited to the 40th Flatcoat Retriever Society annual Breed show, where Barney was a guest of honour. It was a very special day in many ways as we met up with Barney's original owner who filled us in on his early days. One surprise to us was to learn that he had come second in his group at Crufts when he was a one year old!

6 years on…

Thankfully, Archie was finally declared free of cancer at the Royal Children's Hospital Melbourne in June 2018. He couldn't have been better cared for during those 2 years of intensive treatment.

Now at 8 years old, he attends school and growing at a pace along with his older brothers.

* The Skye Trail and the Sutherland Trail.

Barney

Barney is no longer with us having made his last mountain walk in late 2019. Old age caught up with him unfortunately although you wouldn't have known it on Ben Hee in northern Scotland, where he found a patch of snow to roll in, after having climbed the 2500 or so feet to the summit. From here we all sat and looked down at the remote wet 'n wild lands we walked across 5 years ago. We could see Ben More Assynt, Glen Cassley and the river and lochs, and there, the tiny white dot of the Crask Inn standing out amidst all the brown boggy landscape. What memories we shared.

Soon after however, it was clear he was suffering a condition which he was not to recover from.

After the loss of Barney we decided not to get another dog immediately. However, 6 months on, we found ourselves in a very different world with all the restrictions and limitations imposed on us by Covid-19. We decided to contact Brian from whom we originally obtained Barney, (and who walked with us on the start of the Pennine Way) to find out if any flatcoat breed rescue dogs were available.

1 year old Monty

Finding another Barney was unlikely, but as it turned out, Brian and his wife Jane had one puppy unexpectedly available from the litter they had just bred. Here was a rare chance to have a dog from a very well respected and sought after line. We deliberated over whether to take on the challenge of a young flatcoat puppy, as it is a major commitment. The decision was soon made and we now have a young and very playful Monty demanding lots of our time, attention and walks. He hasn't tried backpacking yet.

Highs and Lows

On the penultimate day of the trek, Wendy asked what we considered to be the overall highs and lows. We were probably unable to answer this properly at the time. 6 years on however and perhaps now we can…

Jos's Reflections

Rereading my diaries, writing this book, looking back on our adventurous long walk, in answer to Wendy's question. what were the best, the worst bits, for me, I loved the whole back packing experience, the simple rhythm of life, going to sleep in a tent listening to sounds of nature, wind, rain, running water. waking up to the birds, packing up, loading your rucksack and setting off again, new landscapes ahead to walk in, nature to notice. Until, end of day, time to find a pitch, put our home up, relax, make tea, read, write, paint, explore. Next day, do it all again.

The lowest point of the trip, was the phone call on the cliffs when we learnt about Archie's cancer, then the ongoing worry and uncertainty, his tests, treatment, would he survive? when shall we stop walking to go out to help our Oz family. Walking helped me keep going through this awful time.

The high points for me were the sense of exhilaration felt on reaching high tops, cliffs, hills, ridges, where we enjoyed the panoramic views of the countryside, I loved reaching Scotland and our wild camping/walking in remote areas.

Writing the book inspires me to want to do it all again or another long walking journey. But there's always the opposing desire, home and away. The urge to explore and keep moving versus the feeling for home, being rooted in a place, keeping a garden, knowing a place intimately through the seasons.

A big difference now are 5 more grandchildren, all living locally. I love being part of their lives, The pandemic has reinforced thoughts of never taking things for granted, and to make the most of family and friends (and health while you've still got it)

AND… do the things you want to do while you still can!

Bob's Reflections

We travelled out to Australia soon after finishing the trek without having time to fully appreciate what we had achieved.

As Jos has mentioned, it was quite a shock to hear about Archie soon after we started the trek having previously thought he had a nasal polyp.

Blisters. The situation we found ourselves in on Exmoor was depressing. To find yourself walking slower and slower with so many miles to go felt bleak at the time.

Illness. Going down with coughs and colds just before we reached home made for a few uncomfortable days walking.

And the high points...

The help we received from so many family and friends, no more so than our unplanned stop in Dorset with Penny & Tim, getting through the Scottish Central Belt with John & Penny and the final stages with Geoff & Wendy.

The pleasure we gained from our involvement with Guide Dogs – an unexpected bonus. Hearing first hand from people who have directly benefited from the charity we were supporting inspired us. Also meeting so many dedicated staff and volunteers.

Success in route planning. Our change to the published route through the Scottish Highlands was an unknown. It was satisfying to get to Fort William via our more remote alternative.

The realisation late on that we could complete the trek having had the expectation of an early finish in order to fly out to Australia.

Completing the route through the Flow Country and on to the end, indeed the whole route, largely off road – we really don't like hard, flat surfaces to walk on.

Loads

We kept our loads as light as possible to at least give us a chance of completing the route.

Approximate weights					
Item	**Bob**	**Jos**	**Item**	**Bob**	**Jos**
Tent	3030		Overtrousers	360	284
Cooking	80	820	Jacket	520	488
Bed	590	615	LiteSpeed	190	167
Sleeping Bag + Liner	825	776	Hat	69	70
Torch + batteries	117	117	Gloves	95	70
First Aid kit	190	100	Warm top	334	330
Compass, whistles	40	40	T shirt*	100	86
Toiletry	130	60	Outer socks	70	140
Towel	94	51	Inner socks	66	44
Sigg	150	150	Underwear	90	56
Water Filter	145	115	Radio		100
GPS & case	318	100	Kindle	289	289
GPS Batteries	320	320	Charger + leads	200	
Camera & case	464	280	Power Bank	330	
Camera batteries	102	63	Art materials	500	900
Phone	141	215	PLB	152	
Rucksack	1250	1300	Other (Kg)	2	2

Total: Bob 12Kg, Jos 10Kg

Numbers varied at different stages due to changing loads.

Food and water added up to 4Kg each

Barney carried up to 3.5Kg

* Guide Dogs T shirt to advertise the charity when required.

Our day to day clothes were (all lightweight):

- Marino wool base layer
- Fleece
- Zip off trousers
- Underwear
- 2 pairs of socks, lightweight inner and walking outer
- Walking boots and gaiters

Overtrousers, jackets, hats and gloves included above were worn regularly.

All who Helped

We had substantial help from family and friends without which we wouldn't have managed this trip. Although we organised the trek as a self-supporting backpacking trip, the reality is that much help is actually needed.

- Rosie & Garry. Starting us off from home, meeting up at Monmouth and a glorious afternoon at Burnlaw as we neared home.
- Nigel, Kay and guide dog Jackie. At the very start and then a complete surprise at the very end!
- Keith & Margaret. Our first rest day and a chance to chill out on the Cornish Riviera. and meet up with family over the Easter weekend.
- John & Liz at Huntstile Organic Farm for saving the day when the local pub turned us away.
- Penny & Tim. After struggles with blisters we were treated to a holiday with old friends from Settlingstones who couldn't do enough for us – a wonderful time recuperating and reminiscing.
- Richard & Emma. Our bags were carried for a stage and a welcome night indoors in an area that had hit the headlines not long ago for the severe floods.
- Karolie. We met en route in Cornwall. Karolie (and her lovely golden retrievers) offered to put us up when we reached Cheddar. A welcome change from camping.
- Poppy. We needed somewhere to stay around Bristol and pick up one of our resupply parcels – a vital point in the journey.
- Mick, Penny, Ian, Stephen and Geraldine. Worcester family – picked up, resupply, family gathering and then return to the trail lightly loaded. Walked with family and we even got lost!
- Hilary & Mike. Old friends put us up and Hilary walked a stage with us on another lightly loaded stage. Thanks to Mike for the driving.
- Robin & Gwynn. Again, old friends who went out of their way – Jos needed new boots and we did a mini tour of Sheffield outdoor shops. Another stage with only day sacks and at last we're in the Pennines. One of the places we simply have to return to – we want to ascend Mam Tor in clear conditions!
- Joanna & Phil. Our vital resupply before we tackled 'England's Last Wilderness' here in the North Pennines.
- Mick & Ann. Baggage transfer while we walked with just day sacks.
- Jane & Neil. Walking with us and looking after Barney after we had finished.
- John & Angie. Even though off to France the next day we had somewhere to stay after finishing the Pennine Way.
- John & Penny. The section difficult for accommodation. We were taken back and forth to near Sterling whilst we were able to walk several stages light loaded.

- Geoff & Wendy. Help at Fort William and then we met up again at the Crask Inn where Wendy and Meg walked with us to the end while Geoff ferried gear, appeared en route with cups of tea, ice creams and other wonderful treats.
- Sue. Picked us up from Haltwhistle station and took us home (at last).
- Lorraine and the rest of the Dogs Unite team at Reading for the organising and support throughout.
- Nikky, Julie and Fionna from Guide Dogs Scottish central belt where we were treated like royalty!
- Pippa, Guide Dogs back home and a party was arranged at short notice in our local pub.

We camped for most of the trip so the Inns and Hotels we chose had to be special. All are wholeheartedly recommended, are dog friendly and deserve a visit...

- The Red Lion Hotel, Clovelly
- The Royal Oak, Luxborough
- The Notley Arms Inn, Monksilver
- Tan Hill Inn, North Yorkshire Dales
- The Crask Inn, Sutherland

Donations

The response to our walk was truly outstanding. As well as collecting directly as we walked, we had over 250 donations online at our JustGiving page and through our text donations number. Many thanks to all of you.

A special thanks must go to:

- The Flat Coat Retriever Society who were so generous with two substantial donation. (You can see a picture of Barney relaxing by the fire in his new home here on the Rescue Rehousing page)
- Our son-in-law's firm, Grontmij whose Newcastle workforce made collections every week for the duration of the trip.
- Hadrian Vets, Hexham. Not only looking after Barney but adding a substantial customer collection to our total.

With these additions, we raised a total of £8000. The Dogs Unite ' Match a Mile for Barney' scheme raised more than £22000 with over 1200 people and dogs taking part!

A number of organisations reduced or waived fees when they found out we were associated with a charity. Equivalent sums were added to the donations total. In all cases, people were generous and couldn't have been more helpful. Apologies for any missing entries...

- The North Inn, Pendeen – good collection in pub to start us off
- Porthbeach Holiday Park, Newquay
- Porthtowan Holiday Park – made welcome even though the site was still officially shut.
- Atlantic View Caravan Park, Portcothan and Porthconan Bay Stores
- Cabin Cafe, Crackington Haven. Not a campsite but the owner let us camp in her garden. Also the offer of phoning Australia as we had an urgent need to contact relatives.
- Greencliff Farm, Bideford. The owner's son kindly did some shopping for us as no shops were nearby and we were staying 2 nights.
- Brightlycott Barton campsite, Barnstaple. One of our pre-planned packages was waiting for us.
- Huntstile Organic Farm – rescued us after torrential rain when it was getting too dangerous to walk on the unlit roads. We were well fed and had an exceptional room on the house for the night.
- Totney Farm, Mark. We decided to have a short day but it meant a long detour by road to get to the campsite. A farmer stopped and after chatting, suggested we take a short cut through his land which saved us many miles of road walking.
- Oak Farm campsite, Congresbury
- Celia of Canine Relate near the Severn Bridge. Looking for somewhere to pitch a tent and we were able to stay in a field belonging to Celia where she instructs owners and trains dogs – Barney was at home!
- Eve Victoria Cafe, Hay on Wye. Even though they were closing, we were presented with tea and cakes just when we needed it most.
- Radnors End Campsite, Hay on Wye
- The Copper Kettle, Much Wenlock. A welcome break and then they collected on our behalf.
- Wenlock Hardware, Much Wenlock for the replacement sleeping mat for Barney.
- Darbys, Ironbridge
- Tong Hill Farm, Tong Norton. A farmer offered the use of his garden for camping.
- Cannock Chase Camping and Caravanning Club campsite
- The Dapple Grey, Uttoxeter. A very busy Sunday afternoon after race day but once the staff knew we were collecting for Guide Dogs they couldn't do enough for us.
- Ashbourne Heights Country Park, Thorpe
- The Rambler Inn, Edale
- Carrylite Baggage Transfer Service. No we didn't use the service! We met on St Cuthbert's Way and the driver donated and offered us their service should we need it.
- Jedburgh campsite
- Linwater campsite
- Campsie Pharmacy, Milton of Campsie
- Cobleland Campsite, Aberfoyle
- Ewen's Taxis, Ullapool